## DATE DUE

| | |
|---|---|
| MAR 1 5 2001 | |
| | |
| NOV 2 7 2002 | |
| | |
| | |
| | |
| | |
| | |
| | |
| | |
| | |
| | |

BRODART, CO.                    Cat. No. 23-221-003

# Dilemmas in American Politics

Series Editor   **L. Sandy Maisel,** *Colby College*

Dilemmas in American Politics offers teachers and students a series of quality books on timely topics and key institutions in American government. Each text will examine a "real world" dilemma and will be structured to cover the historical, theoretical, policy relevant, and future dimensions of its subject.

## BOOKS IN THIS SERIES

# Remote & Controlled

........................................................

## Media Politics in a Cynical Age

SECOND EDITION

**Matthew Robert Kerbel**
*Villanova University*

Westview Press
A Member of the Perseus Books Group

*Dilemmas in American Politics*

Copyright © 1999 by Westview Press, A Member of the Perseus Books Group

Published in 1999 in the United States of America by Westview Press, 5500 Central Avenue, Boulder, Colorado 80301-2877, and in the United Kingdom by Westview Press, 12 Hid's Copse Road, Cumnor Hill, Oxford OX2 9JJ

Library of Congress Cataloging-in-Publication Data
Kerbel, Matthew Robert, 1958–
    Remote and controlled : media politics in a cynical age / Matthew
Robert Kerbel. — 2nd ed.
        p.   cm. — (Dilemmas in American politics)
    Includes bibliographical references (p.   ) and index.
    ISBN 0-8133-6869-3
    1. Mass media—Political aspects—United States.   2. United
States—Politics and government—20th  century.   I. Title.
II. Series.
P95.82.U6K47   1999
302.23'0973—dc21                                                                 98-35203
                                                                                              CIP

The paper used in this publication meets the requirements of the American National Standard for Permanence of Paper for Printed Library Materials Z39.48-1984.

10     9     8     7     6     5     4     3     2     1

*For Gabrielle, with the wish that her generation*
*may find a way to renew optimism, excitement, and hope*

# Contents

# 4   Presidential Governance and Other Fantasies                             101

# 5   What About Us?                                                          131

# Illustrations

# Preface and Acknowledgments

It probably shouldn't have surprised me. After all, I knew doubts about government ran fairly deep. Still, I couldn't quite shake the memory of the response I got from the students in my introductory American Government class when I asked how many of them trusted politicians, at least some of the time. No hands went up. Not one. And this was a fairly talkative group. For the most part sophomores, they had concluded by age twenty that little good could be expected from people who had made a career of public service. The verdict was unanimous. And they are not alone. Surveys show that their opinions mirror larger national attitudes, albeit to an extreme degree. It wasn't always like this. Why is it now?

Shortly thereafter, "Meet the Press" hosted Bush White House Chief of Staff Samuel Skinner. Things were not upbeat in the Bush administration at the time. Nor were they pleasant on the Sunday program, as Skinner was pelted with acerbic questions of dubious value to anyone outside the administration. Were his views on key social issues different from the president's? How could he claim to be competent when the White House was so disorganized? Why were people in the administration saying nasty things about his capability behind his back?

The reporters asking these questions know better than anyone that administration officials were undermining Skinner because the White House is staffed by people with huge egos, a variety of personal beliefs, and their own agendas. There is always disorganization, and people backbite. The presumption underlying the reporters' questions troubled me as much as the reaction to politicians I had gotten from my sophomores. Do we really want perfection to be the standard against which journalists measure our politicians and political organizations? Show me an institution that does run smoothly, where everyone is of like mind, where all motives are pure. A university, perhaps? A television newsroom?

Reporters could say that government is different, that public officials should be held to a higher standard, given how their actions affect hundreds of millions of people in this country and potentially billions abroad. That is precisely why exchanges like the one on "Meet the Press" are so disconcerting. High standards are important, but impossible standards can foster an endless, dubious, presumptuous dialogue between reporters and political figures that makes it easy to tear down politicians in the name of protecting the rest of us.

I kept thinking about my sophomores. They didn't have to watch "Meet the Press" to get the message—it's pervasive. In newspapers and on broadcast and cable television, on talk radio, even on computer conferences, it is hard to escape the idea that politicians are not to be trusted, that politics is played primarily for self-gain, that no one is any good. This seemed to me more than the reflection of a healthy skepticism of the sort with long roots in our rebellious culture. I began to wonder about the relationship between these two things, between my turned-off sophomores and "Meet the Press," about how it is possible for us to educate ourselves to the ways of government without acquiring the journalist's cynical pose. At the nexus of political learning and political involvement lies the dilemma we will discuss here. Democracy is problematic without knowledge, but it is equally problematic without participation. Is there a way to survive the bombardment of cynical coverage and still feel the desire to be part of the process?

Three years later, as I prepare the second edition of this book, these concerns remain relevant. As the class of 2000 struggles with finding a way to accept the political system without being repelled by it, national political coverage continues to be unhelpful. The announcement that President Clinton may have had an affair with a White House intern and obstructed justice by asking her to lie about it under oath sparked the press's engagement in a self-indulgent orgy of speculation in which even respectable commentators salivated over the prospect that the charges would claim a presidential scalp. We were treated to coverage of politics as blood sport where the juiciness of the allegations and the amount of power at stake impelled reporters to indulge in sloppy coverage that sometimes confused innuendo with fact.

Given this irresponsible coverage, one may be tempted to place blame for the dilemma with the media. But to do so would be simplistic. How politics gets covered is inseparable from how it is conducted. Important changes—particularly in technology and institutional reform—have made political actors into free agents and brought the rough-and-tumble of politics to the fore. The present system confers benefits on presidents and representatives, their political operatives, interest groups, journalists, and virtually every insider with political aspirations or power. Quite possibly, the long-term erosion of faith in the political process is the cost of preserving these players' short-term benefits. But delineating this dilemma is not the same as saying the press is behaving poorly. We will consider what the press contributes to the dilemma in this broader context. This is not another media-bashing book; there are enough of those.

As the second edition of this work nears production, I would like to thank those who generously contributed their time and ideas so that a manuscript could become a book: Karen O'Connor, John Bibby, Craig Rimmerman, Ruth Jones, Diana Evans, Ronald Rapoport, Nelson Polsby, David Canon, Linda Fowler, Larry Sabato, Hugh Jones, and John Coleman. Through their invaluable editorial supervision, Sandy Maisel and Jennifer Knerr helped to develop and shape core elements of the first edition of this book while giving me their constant encouragement. Leo Wiegman did the same for the second edition. At Westview, Eric Wright and Brenda Hadenfeldt worked tirelessly to move early drafts of this work through production. And, as always, Adrienne Adler Kerbel lovingly offered unending patience, support, and editorial guidance. Although I retain full responsibility for the contents of this book, it is a far better work because of their efforts than it otherwise would have been.

*Matthew Robert Kerbel*
Villanova, Pennsylvania

# 1

......................................................................................

# Introduction:
# Under the
# President's Clothes

The exchange between the young woman and
the president of the United States went like this:

Woman: The world is dying to know:
   Is it boxers or briefs?
The President: Briefs, usually.

WITH THAT, PRESIDENT CLINTON REVEALED his underwear preferences, both to the seventeen-year-old questioner and to anyone in the country who happened to be watching. Because this dialogue happened in a television studio, was broadcast on MTV,[1] and was subsequently reported on television and in the newspapers, countless millions of Americans became privy to information about the president's drawers.

Several years after this 1994 exchange, the most remarkable thing about it is that it doesn't seem remarkable. The most personal details about our public figures—from what the president wears under his pants to what behaviors he allegedly does and does not consider adulterous—are routinely available to us on television, in print, and on the Web. We may even consider it within our right to know the most intimate facts about the famous and the powerful. This is a relatively recent phenomenon. Try to imagine Richard Nixon or Jimmy Carter answering the question Clinton was asked.

As difficult as it may be to believe in this era of frenzied publicity, until very recently, the manner in which politicians made and reporters covered the news precluded such a public discussion from happening. Media, for the most part, came in four traditional forms: newspapers, magazines, network television, and radio. A typical news consumer in 1975 probably could select among a local newspaper (and, if ambitious, a paper from a business or political capital, such as the *New York Times* or the *Washington Post*), a news-magazine like *Time* or *Newsweek,* local and network television news programs, and possibly a newsradio channel. These sources would present the news in varying degrees of detail, but private, prurient topics were relegated to sleazy tabloids.

Consequently, it is hard to imagine a head of state twenty years ago addressing a forum in which intimate questions might be asked. In fact, it is difficult even to imagine what such a forum would have looked like: Before MTV and before the proliferation of cable channels, there was no **medium** through which an elected official could submit to direct public questioning of the sort President Clinton faced from his young audience.

But times have changed. The number of information outlets has exploded, and each additional forum has produced new opportunities for politicians to reach out to constituents, sometimes in unconventional ways. In one version of the new media, political leaders like President Clinton face the public directly, without benefit of reporters; this type of arrangement produced the underwear discussion. The forum was Music Television—a cable channel developed for amusement, not politics. That a president finds MTV a worthwhile vehicle for reaching a slice of the electorate is as indicative of the changing shape of media politics as is the fact that MTV regularly presents its own news reports, from which a large share of people under thirty get their news.

The opportunities provided politicians by new information vehicles like MTV have redrawn the parameters of political activity—and political coverage. The volume of information available to us is staggering. Politicians now seem to be all over the place, at one minute appearing on a television talk show, the next minute beaming their likeness via satellite for a brief appearance on your local newscast. News reporters keep pace, digesting material from this highly charged political world and presenting it—quickly—in a summary form that contextualizes it for viewers and readers.

We might think the availability of all this information would make people feel closer to Washington and in tune with public officials. After all, if Americans wish to learn about government, partake in political discourse, or even become political junkies, there has never been a period in our history in which proximity to politics was any more convenient. Just turn on the television, power up the computer, or pick up a newspaper. Ours is a world where easy access could mean ready involvement and the tremendous sense of efficacy that comes from playing a role in a representative system.

Clearly this is not happening. To the contrary, large numbers of Americans feel detached from those running the country. As a nation, we are skeptical of the motives of government officials and cynical about the possibility that they can perform admirably. Trust in government lingers at an all-time low, and politician is a dirty word. If anything, familiarity with the political system appears to breed contempt.

Why is this? After all, the exercise of power that is and always has been an essential component of self-governance need not be regarded disparagingly, even if it contains manipulative elements. For centuries, advancement of the collective good has occurred as a product of self-interested individuals exercising influence. In this respect, power politics is more aptly described as necessary and important than as good or bad. But that is not how many people regard it.

Public reliance on television has climbed as trust in government has fallen, so it is convenient to say that the media should be blamed for this decline in trust. But that response is overly simplistic. In fact, we will see how a host of players contribute to a steady supply of cynical messages about contemporary politics. Political actors in the executive and legislative branches, candidates who would like to serve in those branches, interest-group representatives, and the press all benefit from newfound opportunities for the advancement of self-interest made possible through changes in how presidents govern, how Congress operates, how national campaigns are run, and how the press covers politics. This condition makes the self-serving nature of politics more paramount than it was in the past and presents the public with good reasons to feel turned off to government.

For a sense of this, just look at the mediated messages about politics and politicians that encrust objective information about what happened to whom, where, and when. The news we receive is replete with cynical doings once known only to insiders. For instance, on the same day as the underwear encounter, the *Los Angeles Times* ran a story about rumors claiming White House Chief of Staff Thomas F. "Mack" McLarty was in danger of being replaced—a sign of administration weakness in the world of Washington but hardly a fact the nation needed to know. The piece quoted Clinton aides as saying they had undertaken a "quiet effort to counter perceptions" that McLarty lacked the knowledge and authority to perform his functions effectively. The story straightforwardly recounted efforts that could be considered manipulative ("trying to show off McLarty's firm side") or even deceptive ("promoting news stories that portray McLarty as asserting stronger control over staff operations"). Power politics, of course, is not new. But detailed attention to such internal posturing was once not provided to those looking on at home. Something has changed, bringing behind-the-scenes actions to the center of public attention.

The media are accurate to question the motivation of the political figures they portray, but self-promotion is only one of a variety of apt perspectives for politics. It may alternatively be described as a noble profession, in which difficult decisions are made in the effort to govern large numbers of people. Whereas *politician* is an ugly word to many, *statesman* has a far more admirable ring. But how many people do we see depicted as statesmen on television? The politicians who provide the daily staple of media coverage seem to spend much of their day maneuvering others to maximize personal interests. This is because they are frequently depicted in terms of the gritty, problematic process of running for office or passing legislation—a process that has become far more accessible and visible in recent years and that, like sausage making, can be an unpleasant thing to watch closely. Reporters watch it all the time—and fill in the gory details.

If such ungainly news items were simply one aspect of what we heard about major league politics, this still might be an insignificant matter. But there is a larger problem: In order to help us make sense of the vast quantities of information conveyed every day, the media supply us with a framework much like the theme of the McLarty story for understanding what politics is about and how government operates. We are prompted to think about the political system as the journalist tells us about it, as a place filled with people of dubious character bent on image manipulation at all costs. It becomes a challenge for us to sort out political information in the news from messages about the political system conveyed along with the facts—to learn about politics without acquiring an attitude. To seek political data in the midst of the information revolution is often to find wary messages about the people who run our democracy.

This causes a dilemma: Given how the media portray political information, how can we expect to be informed without feeling alienated? Assuming we wish to be knowledgeable about politics and government, how can we wade through the bundles of information available to us without succumbing to the distrustful messages that often accompany it? We will explore this dilemma by looking at how politics and government are portrayed by the media in general and by television in particular. In the process, we will uncover the intricate set of relationships between journalists and the political figures they cover, each of whom contributes to how news is reported. We will try to discern the reasons political information is distilled by the doubts of those who report it—reasons that reach far beyond the press to include elected officials, political institutions, and quite possibly those of us in the audience who consume the news.

## How We Respond to the Message

Strong claims will be made in the pages that follow about the political messages found in the media. If the messages are to be of concern to us, we first need to establish how they affect their intended audience, the mass public. There is evidence of several types of influence. One widely accepted consequence of watching television news and reading newspapers is the tendency for people to begin to think about the things addressed in the media. In other words, if news reports focus heavily on the subject of crime, people who pay attention to those reports may find themselves thinking about the issue of crime and believing that it is an important concern. This effect is called **agenda setting** because the impact of the media is felt on the makeup of the public agenda, the things we are aware of and think are significant.

Evidence supporting the agenda-setting effect of the mass media has been around for a long time, although some media scholars have called into question the extent of the effect. Early agenda-setting studies documented a relationship between public awareness of news items and their prominence in the media, but it was entirely possible that news coverage was simply reflecting preexisting public concerns (McCombs and Shaw, 1972). More recent research underscores the early assertion that media coverage can have a sizable impact on the public agenda under the right circumstances. One study demonstrates a close relationship between the importance placed on public issues by a panel of news consumers and the prominence of those issues in newspapers and on television (Graber, 1988). Another finds that commentators and expert sources appearing in the news influence viewers through the enhanced credibility that comes with their authoritative position (Page et al., 1987). However, the agenda-setting effect may be weak when people already have strong opinions about an issue, or when the concerns expressed in news reports diverge sharply from the concerns of readers and viewers (Neuman et al., 1992; Graber, 1988).

Note that agenda setting doesn't extend to the specific opinions people hold on a particular issue. Influencing what people think *about* is entirely different from influencing the manner in which people think. So although we might attribute widespread concern with crime to the agenda-setting effect of the mass media, we would be hard-pressed to argue on the basis of agenda setting alone that media exposure leads us to specific conclusions about what needs to be done about crime. After all, drawing conclusions is a complex procedure that could be affected by our preexisting opinions on the subject, the views of our friends and relatives, book knowledge—indeed, myriad non-media-related influences.

But there is compelling evidence that on political and social matters, television structures how we think about things through the context in which information is presented. By drawing attention to select political circumstances, television primes the viewer on how to think about the news. This **priming** effect works in a subtle way to influence the framework by which we understand the political world, particularly how we think about the performance of public figures (Iyengar and Kinder, 1987). For instance, stories portraying President Clinton in the context of his unsuccessful and largely unpopular campaign to revamp the health care system could prime the viewer toward a negative appraisal of the president. Coverage that emphasizes the success of his efforts to win congressional approval for the North American Free Trade Agreement might lead to an entirely different set of assessments.

Because it is simpler to photograph individuals than abstractions and because concrete events are easy to communicate in words, television reports prime us to experience news as a personalized entity, often reducing complicated story lines to tangible, easily communicated episodes while avoiding complex explanations for political phenomena. This episodic approach is attractive to television reporters, because it doesn't require great expertise in the structural correlates of poverty to write, say, a story about a specific welfare recipient. Arguably, however, this approach makes it hard for us to reason intelligently about what we see, to consider the complex relationships among the disparate dramas that compose television news. At its most far-reaching, episodic coverage may undermine our ability to make meaningful assessments of politics and policy, such as how politicians address political problems (Iyengar, 1996).

Note how the priming effect is addressed in terms of television. In the words of one research team that has studied the medium extensively, television is "more attention-grabbing, emotional, surprising, interesting, and personally relevant" than either newspapers or magazines (Neuman et al., 1992: p. 59).[2] These qualities make television particularly important to our understanding of the role played by the media in **political socialization,** or the manner in which our attitudes toward and opinions of politics and government are shaped and developed.

Political socialization begins when we are children and continues throughout our adult lives. Along with family, friends, and teachers, television reaches deeply into the lives of young people, influencing what they know and how they feel about the political system. Initially, these feelings tend to be positive and supportive, particularly toward basic values such as freedom of expression and tolerance of others. With the onset of adolescence, however, teenagers tend to become skeptical about politics. The impact of television at this point in development is less clear.

However, it is well established that television viewing continues ritualistically for most adults, perpetuating the role of the medium in the lifelong learning process. Most Americans today spend half their free time watching television, during which time they are exposed to a vast amount of information on events they otherwise would know nothing about (Stanley and Niemi, 1988). As political attitudes stabilize in adulthood, television viewing remains a rich resource for learning about new political occurrences and refining established attitudes.

Even if television plays an important role in socialization for many people, we are not affected uniformly by media use. **Demographic factors,** or group characteristics such as race, gender, age, and education, may influence the kind of exposure we get to political messages and the manner in which we process them. African Americans and Hispanics rely less than whites on television and newspapers as a source of information and tend to prefer to get news from ethnically oriented media. Older women watch more television news than any other group; teenagers watch the least. Better-educated individuals tend to read more and may be better able to think critically about the messages contained in the news (Graber, 1993; Miller et al., 1979).

But the more we watch television, the more likely we are to develop perceptions of the political and social world that conform to the messages conveyed by the medium and the less likely we are to subscribe to the beliefs and attitudes of light viewers of similar age, education, income, or other demographics. This development of a common set of values among heavy television viewers, called **main-streaming,** is powerful evidence that repeated exposure to television programming, as one research team puts it, "virtually monopolizes and subsumes other sources of information, ideas, and consciousness" (Gerbner et al., 1980a: p. 14).

The effect has been demonstrated with respect to a variety of social and political concerns. Heavy television viewers tend to call themselves political moderates, assuming a conventional, middle-of-the-road perspective that parallels the values portrayed in the medium (Gerbner et al., 1982; 1984). But because the messages on television are mixed, heavy viewers also, in the words of one observer, "think like conservatives and want like liberals" (Morgan, 1989). This confusion manifests itself in attitudes and behaviors that make it hard for officials to govern, as people in this group are more likely than light viewers to distrust government and refrain from voting yet are more likely to demand government assistance and protection.

The mistrusting attitudes follow from media messages that emphasize the failure of politicians to respond to public needs. The greater demands are the product of messages that inflate the magnitude of danger we face in our daily lives. Heavy viewers, for instance, are more likely to overestimate the presence of violence in society, in keeping with television's tendency to overrepresent violent acts, and to adhere to television's marginal view of the elderly and their living conditions (Gerbner et al., 1980a; 1980b). Other skewed social attitudes may also be traced to television messages. Female viewers of high socioeconomic status who regularly watch television and who otherwise would not be expected to hold sexist opinions have been found to express attitudes reflecting the marginal presentation of women on television. Heavy viewers even express attitudes toward doctors and lawyers that mirror the messages appearing on air (Morgan, 1982; Volgy and Schwarz, 1980; Carlson, 1985).

In each instance, differences in perceptions of the political or social environment that would be expected given cultural or social differences among viewers disappear in the wake of heavy television consumption. This is particularly important to the dilemma we will be exploring, because we will assume that people need to be fairly regular media consumers in order to be informed. What does this mean? At best, frequent television viewers are consuming confusing, skewed, and unrealistic accounts of politics and society. At worst, these problematic messages may be undermining public support for democracy and its processes, potentially putting support for the political system at risk (Morgan, 1989). This gives us good reason to look closely at the essence and caliber of the information available to us as we develop our perceptions of politics and government. In particular, it gives us cause to look closely at the messages contained on television, that most ubiquitous of information sources.

## Where We Get the Message

Think for a second of all the sources of information that did not exist when to-day's twenty-year-olds were born. To the local newspaper, add *USA Today,* which accurately bills itself as a national newspaper by virtue of satellite technology that beams it across the entire country for assembly and sale in hundreds of local markets. To local radio news add call-in talk radio programs. Then there is television. Local news programs still air at 6:00 and 11:00 P.M. eastern time (although in many cities, they're longer than they were twenty years ago). Peter Jennings, Tom Brokaw, and Dan Rather anchor the network evening news in a format that resembles television news from 1975. But there are newer options as well. On any given night, viewers can find at least one network newsmagazine (whereas twenty years ago, "60 Minutes" on CBS was the pioneer of a fairly new format). ABC's "Nightline," a program born of coverage of the Iranian hostage crisis in the Carter administration, appears five evenings a week following late local news. Cable offers substantial coverage. CNN operates two around-the-clock news channels, including a headline service. C-SPAN channels televise the House of Representatives and Senate, where two decades ago cameras were strictly forbidden. CNBC offers business and political news and commentary. One cable channel devotes itself entirely to talk. And, of course, there is MTV news.

To this mix add the Internet explosion, which over the past few years has overwhelmed us with information. Armed with a good browser, those with access to a personal computer and a telephone line can find electronic editions of major newspapers, copies of White House policy initiatives, the voting records of their elected representatives, and a numbing assortment of other data. Hybrid media, like the Microsoft-NBC partnership, MSNBC, enhance the network's news offerings by giving Net surfers the chance to interface with guests, get follow-up information on broadcast stories, and read the latest headlines as they are updated.

Although Internet usage is still quite limited, the effect of the proliferation of media has been the emergence of more unconventional venues for political discourse. Many Americans listen to talk radio hosts like Rush Limbaugh. Their television counterparts occasionally deal in political information as well, such as during the 1992 campaign when Phil Donahue hosted a "debate" on his daytime program between Democratic presidential candidates Bill Clinton and Jerry Brown. Larry King hosts a television talk show that routinely attracts major political figures, to whom audience members can pose questions if they are lucky enough to reach the studio switchboard. Tabloid programs resembling moving versions of checkout stand gossip magazines dot the television landscape, serving up the sordid side of public life with an anchor-based format reminiscent of the local news. Even pure entertainment programs have become sources for political information. When the Clinton administration announced its plans for reducing the size of the federal government in 1993, Vice President Al Gore appeared on "Late Show with David Letterman" to share a few laughs—and to promote the administration's initiative. Similarly, after Bob Dole lost the 1996 presidential election, he made the round of late-night comedy shows, acting more like a triumphant celebrity than a vanquished candidate.

Unquestionably, television is the principal source of political information. For the population as a whole, television use has skyrocketed over the course of the last generation. Since 1970, almost every household in America has reported having at least one television set. Between 1980 and 1992, the percentage of households with cable television climbed steadily every year, from 20 to 60 percent (Stanley and Niemi, 1994).

The trend away from the printed page is equally impressive. In 1986, two-thirds of American households reported using television as their main source of news, whereas newspapers were selected by only 36 percent—down 21 percentage points in twenty-five years.[3] In a 1992 study, 64 percent said they watched television news five or more days during a typical week, compared with only 48 percent who stated they read the newspaper as frequently. Almost one in five claimed never to pick up a newspaper at all (Miller et al., 1993). Likewise, in 1996, 63 percent of respondents to a similar study reported watching television news some of the time or a lot (Miller et al., 1996).

And people profess to be paying attention, particularly to politics. Eighty percent of those questioned in a national survey said they paid at least some regard to news coverage of the 1996 political campaign (Miller et al., 1996), up from seven in ten in 1992. Additionally, in 1992, almost two-thirds recalled watching television programs about the campaign aside from what appeared on news reports (Miller et al., 1993). It seems that television is not simply serving as background noise for other activities; many people are watching and listening to the message.

Perhaps more extraordinary is the change in the respective levels of credibility afforded television and print news. One national survey conducted since 1959 asked this question: "If you got conflicting or different reports of the same news story from radio, television, the magazines, and the newspapers, which of the four versions would you be most inclined to believe?" In 1959, 32 percent of the respondents said newspapers, and only 29 percent selected television. But two years later, television had surpassed newspapers as the most trusted medium (see Figure 1.1). In 1992, 56 percent said they believed television news more than the other media; only one in five selected the papers (Stanley and Niemi, 1994).

11

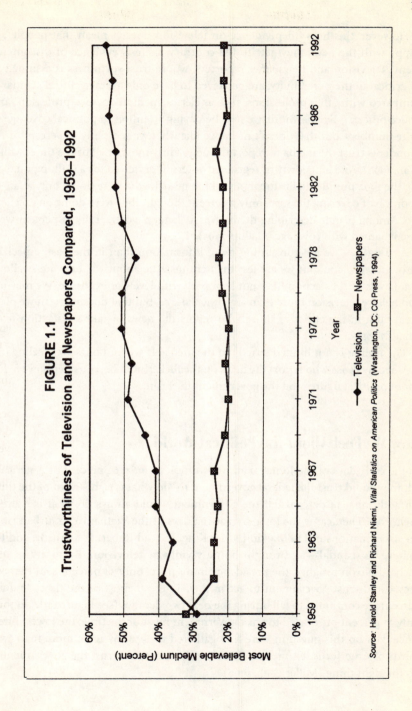

**FIGURE 1.1**

**Trustworthiness of Television and Newspapers Compared, 1959–1992**

*Source:* Harold Stanley and Richard Niemi, *Vital Statistics on American Politics* (Washington, DC: CQ Press, 1994).

However, this heavy dependence on television doesn't mean that people are happy with the news they get. To the contrary, there is evidence of discontentment. Television and newspaper reporters, whose trustworthiness is assumed to be critical to their credibility, are perceived to have only average ethical standards compared with other professions, such as clerics, medical doctors, professors, and police officers.[4] Furthermore, we may be paying attention to political coverage in large numbers, but that doesn't mean we like what we see. Only 37 percent of respondents trust the media to report the news fairly most or all of the time (Miller et al., 1996). And a majority of registered voters interviewed for a Gallup poll during the 1992 presidential campaign said the news media were doing only a fair or poor job of covering the race; only 7 percent thought they were doing an excellent job. Among people describing themselves as "angry" voters, fully 71 percent were disenchanted with coverage (Gallup, 1993).[5]

As a nation, we are consuming more information than in the past, especially through television, but we are less than enthusiastic about what we are swallowing. Levels of satisfaction have not kept pace with levels of exposure. We may use and believe television more than any other source, but that doesn't mean we place great faith in the ethics of those who report the news or take satisfaction from what they say.

The feeling is not limited strictly to the media. If we find ourselves feeling unsatisfied by those who report the news on the flickering tube, consider how we feel about political figures and the government they run.

## How We Feel About the Political World

In the early days of the Johnson administration in 1964, 62 percent of Americans felt they could trust the federal government to "do what is right" most of the time. An additional 14 percent felt the government would always do what is right in their eyes. Then came the long, harrowing days of the Vietnam War, urban riots, the assassinations of Dr. Martin Luther King, Jr., and Robert F. Kennedy, and the Watergate scandal—all brought home vividly by television. By 1974, the year Richard Nixon resigned the presidency in disgrace, only 34 percent said they felt they could trust government to act in their interests most of the time. And the percentage continued to fall during the next two decades (see Figure 1.2).[6] In 1992, only 21 percent purported to trust government most of the time, the lowest figure since data on this question were first gathered in 1958. By 1996, more than two-thirds of Americans felt they never or hardly ever could trust the government to do the right thing (Miller et al., 1996).

13

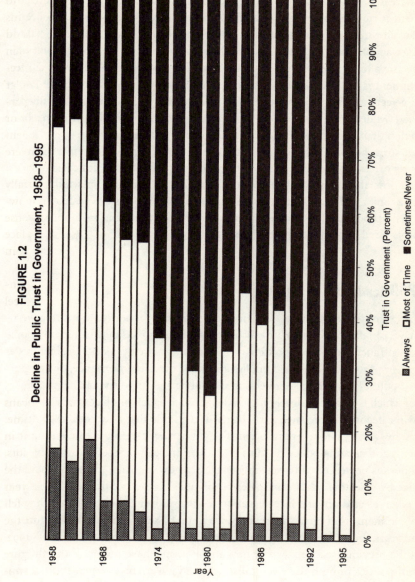

**FIGURE 1.2**
**Decline in Public Trust in Government, 1958–1995**

Trust in Government (Percent)

■ Always □ Most of Time ■ Sometimes/Never

Year

*Source:* George Gallup, Jr., *The Gallup Poll 1996* (Wilmington, DE: Scholarly Resources, Inc., 1997).

Indications of dissatisfaction abound. People are disaffected: Results from the 1996 American National Election Study indicate that almost half of the people feel they have no say about what government does, and almost three in four believe government is run for the benefit of a few big interests rather than for the collective good of all citizens. People are skeptical: Sixty-one percent believe public officials do not care about what citizens think, and the same percentage feel government officials waste a lot of their tax dollars. People are confused: More than six in ten feel government is too complicated for them to understand. People are cynical: Forty-three percent say they believe quite a few government figures could be classified as crooked (Miller et al., 1996). Three-fourths believe elected officials care more about reelection than in doing what is right for the nation (Gallup, 1997).

Not surprisingly, elected officials are not widely regarded as ethical pillars. If news reporters receive average evaluations of their honesty and ethical standards, elected officials rank toward the bottom. Members of Congress place third from last in a ranking of the ethical standards of twenty-six professions evaluated in the 1996 Gallup poll, in the same neighborhood as advertising and insurance agents. Senators fared only slightly better (see Figure 1.3).

## Of Politics and Governance

To the extent that such dissatisfaction finds expression in our reactions to government, we can distinguish two broadly defined political arenas in which many people feel disenfranchised. One is **politics,** or the ongoing activities of political figures as they attempt to attain and hold public office. The other is **governance,** or that portion of politics devoted to representing the public and to policymaking, the objective of which is to debate, develop, and advance social goals or objectives. Obviously, the two categories are related, particularly in the sense that they both speak to the *process* by which political events occur. The governance aspect of representing constituents and creating policy requires politics. In the electoral setting, the objective of politics is power: to win a seat in Congress, a governorship, the presidency, and the like by defeating other candidates at the polls. Power politics also comes into play when elected officials face allegations of inappropriate behavior that threaten to topple them from office, a circumstance faced by several high-profile figures in recent years, including President Clinton and House Speaker Newt Gingrich.

In the previous section, we saw how many people have doubts about the efficacy of politics in both the electoral sphere and governance. When skepticism is expressed about the motives or ethics of public figures, people are saying that politics seems to be a game played strictly for the benefit of the politicians. Likewise,

**FIGURE 1.3**

**Perceived Honesty and Ethical Standards of Media and Government Officials, 1996**

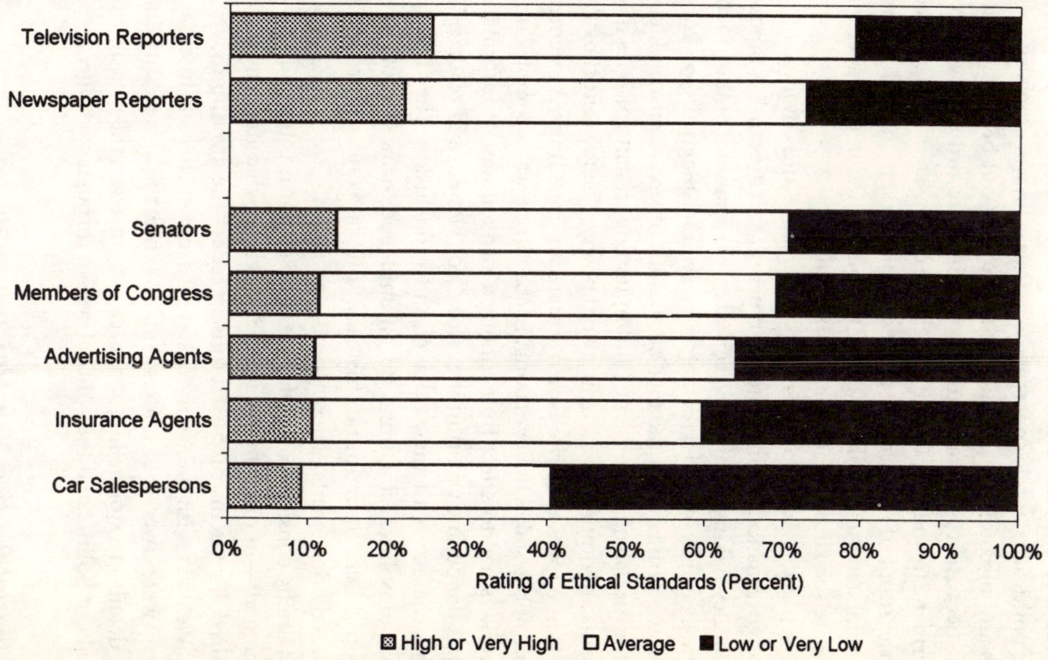

*Source:* George Gallup, Jr., *The Gallup Poll 1996* (Wilmington, DE: Scholarly Resources, 1993).

when people proclaim doubts about the responsiveness of government to their needs, they call into question how effectively political figures are governing.

Both the electoral and governing arenas are subject to great scrutiny in the media messages available to us daily. Consequently, the type of attention given politics and governance in the press should be of particular concern to us if we are to figure out what kind of data inform public attitudes about them. For any given item of political or public concern, the news media will emphasize some facts and themes and discount others. Such selection may not be intentional, but it is inevitable because it is beyond human capacity to record and evaluate all information germane to an issue. Even if the choice of how an issue is covered in the news is not the result of a conscious process, newsworkers through their decisions set the agenda, structure public response to politics, and in a broader sense influence how we are socialized to political phenomena.

In this book, we will consider only the practice and coverage of national politics and governance. To illustrate the types of activities that compose politics and public policymaking at this level, consider two examples of the practice of politics and one example of policymaking. The scandal-plagued 1992 New Hampshire Democratic primary and the 1998 allegations of sexual misconduct and obstruction of justice against President Clinton both represent episodes of the former—politicians attempting to attain and hold power. The 1993 effort by President Clinton to win approval of the North American Free Trade Agreement is a prime example of big-stakes policymaking. Each episode was a complex occurrence, and newsworkers had to select from among a vast amount of information to convey what was happening as a running "story" for viewers and readers. In literature, a story has characters, themes, a climax, and a conclusion. The same applies to news coverage of political situations. But in unfiltered form, this sort of literary structure is nowhere to be found. Instead, political concerns are a hodgepodge of names, activities, events, dates, actions, and words.

Let's briefly consider some of these details—for it is beyond any writer to capture them all—in order to get a general feel for what happened as each incident transpired. The items discussed loosely reflect the attention given them by the media. We will revisit these episodes in subsequent chapters in order to determine how they were covered, to understand how coverage by necessity entailed relating choice details in a storytelling approach, and to assess the messages that were conveyed about politics and the political system through coverage.

## Presidential Politics: New Hampshire, 1992

New Hampshire traditionally holds the nation's first **primary**, the first of many state-by-state contests held in presidential election years for the purpose of selecting **delegates,** or representatives, to the national **political party conventions.** There, the delegates gather to ratify presidential and vice-presidential nominees. Although New Hampshire is small and unrepresentative, the **New Hampshire primary** draws a lot of attention because it is the first test in a primary season that stretches from February to June.

The 1992 New Hampshire primary was held February 18. Although both major parties held primaries on that day, the Democratic primary was more broadly contested because Republicans assumed the incumbent president, George Bush, would easily win renomination by his party. In all, sixty-two self-described Democrats, Republicans, and independents had paid the $1,000 filing fee to appear on the ballot.[7] But only six Democrats received notoriety by virtue of their past or current political positions and well-developed campaign organizations. They were former Governor Edmund G. ("Jerry") Brown of California; Governor Bill Clinton of Arkansas; Iowa Senator Tom Harkin; Nebraska Senator Bob Kerrey; former Senator Paul Tsongas of neighboring Lowell, Massachusetts; and Governor Douglas Wilder of Virginia, who dropped out of the race on January 8.

When Governor Mario Cuomo of New York decided on December 20, 1991, not to run for president, Governor Clinton became the early favorite of political observers and reporters to win the nomination. On several counts, he had successfully done the things winning candidates do. He had garnered the endorsements of Democratic governors, senators, and representatives from all regions of the country. He had attracted campaign advisers with impressive credentials, including highly touted media advisers and fundraisers. And he was raising money. By January, Clinton led all opponents with $581,691 in **federal matching funds**—dollars provided under federal law to match individual contributions up to $250.[8]

In late January, however, a series of setbacks rocked the Clinton campaign. On January 20 the *Star,* a supermarket tabloid, published allegations of extramarital affairs with the candidate by former Arkansas television reporter Gennifer Flowers. Clinton denied the charges, calling them "outright lies" at a January 23 campaign stop in Claremont, New Hampshire. But the story had already been reported in more mainstream media; the *New York Post,* a tabloid newspaper with more legitimacy than the *Star,* ran a screaming headline calling the candidate "Wild Bill," and shortly reporters from many organizations were feeding on Gennifer Flowers material.

At the time, Bill Clinton had been leading his rivals in opinion polls and had been talking at rallies about a set of policy positions: providing universal health care; cutting middle-class taxes by 10 percent; cutting defense spending; and reducing capital gains taxes for small businesses. But after the Flowers allegations, reporters became less interested in covering these matters and more interested in the candidate's personal life. During the week beginning January 23, the three major networks ran a combined 19 stories on the Flowers allegations.[9] In an attempt to defuse the topic, Clinton and his wife, Hillary Rodham Clinton, appeared on the CBS newsmagazine "60 Minutes" on January 26 to discuss their marital history.

Following that appearance, Gennifer Flowers held a press conference that was broadcast live on CNN. She repeated her allegations and played an audiotape of a voice she claimed belonged to Clinton saying, among other things, that Mario Cuomo "acts like" he's in the Mafia. The comment brought a swift rebuke from Cuomo and Senator Kerrey. But opinion polls showed Clinton still leading in New Hampshire.

Then, on February 6, the *Wall Street Journal* reported that Clinton had avoided the draft in 1969 by promising but failing to enroll in an officer-training program. Another round of negative coverage ensued, and this time Clinton's support started to dwindle. Paul Tsongas, a native New Englander who was little more than a curiosity when he first announced his candidacy, started to surface as the **frontrunner** in preelection electoral commentary. Reporters began to see Tsongas as the likely New Hampshire winner and began commenting in news reports that he had emerged as the candidate the others needed to beat. Officials in the Democratic party, worried that the field was weak and leaderless, began to float names of other candidates who might jump into the mix. But the filing deadline for many big-state primaries had already passed, and one by one other would-be candidates declined to run. There was even a write-in effort on behalf of the reluctant Cuomo, but in the end it amounted to very little.

On election day, Tsongas indeed won the New Hampshire primary, garnering 33.2 percent of the vote. Clinton finished second with 24.7 percent. But in the days to come, the Arkansan would turn defeat into victory, calling himself the "comeback kid" who had withstood adversity to finish a strong second. No matter that polls had him solidly in the lead just weeks before: The comeback mantle stuck, and Clinton was on his way to turning what could have been a disappointing New Hampshire loss into subsequent primary wins and eventually into the presidential nomination of his party.

## Scandal, Part Two: Monica Lewinsky, 1998

As president, Bill Clinton continued to face allegations of misdeeds and wrongdoing. His first term was marked by extensive efforts by Kenneth Starr, a special prosecutor appointed by the Justice Department, to look into charges of financial misconduct by the president and first lady stemming from a busted real estate development called Whitewater. The so-called Whitewater prosecutor remained a presence into Clinton's second term, and with a broad grant of authority to investigate the Chief Executive, he expanded his investigation to include matters unrelated to the land deal. But nothing emanating from his investigation would capture the public interest quite like allegations that surfaced in January 1998 that Clinton engaged in a sexual affair with a young White House intern, lied about it under oath, and urged the intern to do the same.

It started with an official denial of the affair by the intern, Monica Lewinsky. She had been asked to testify about her relationship with the president by lawyers for Paula Jones, who had pressed charges against the president in a separate sexual harassment case. Lewinsky's affidavit appeared to contradict statements she had made several months earlier to a colleague, Linda Tripp, in conversations Tripp had secretly recorded. On January 12, five days after Lewinsky made her statement in the Jones case, Tripp informed the special prosecutor about the existence of the tapes, in which she alleged Lewinsky gave details of an affair with the president and told of efforts by Clinton and his confidant Vernon Jordan, a powerful Washington attorney, to get her to lie about it under oath.[10] With Starr's support, Tripp met the next day with Lewinsky and recorded their conversation. Three days later, Starr requested and received formal approval from the Justice Department to expand his probe to investigate the possibility that Clinton had engaged in obstruction of justice in the Jones matter.

The week of January 19 was unlike any Washington had seen for some time, reminding some of the Gennifer Flowers episode, others of the final days of the Nixon administration. It started with a rumor, reported on an Internet gossip page, that *Newsweek* had decided not to publish a story on Lewinsky and her alleged involvement with the president. Within days, that rumor worked its way into mainstream news reports, complete with leaked details of the *Newsweek* piece. On January 21 the story exploded in the mainstream press, with several major news organizations alleging a sexual relationship between the intern and the president, and with Clinton sharply denying the charges. On January 22, Clinton issued a brief but pointed denial of the affair and said he never urged Lewinsky to lie about it. That same day, Jordan sharply denied charges that he had told Lewinsky to lie. Meanwhile, Starr was hard at work expanding his probe into the Lewinsky matter, issuing subpoenas to Clinton's personal secretary and a number of high-ranking administration officials and threatening Lewinsky with prosecution for perjury if she did not appear as a witness against the president. Protracted talks began between Lewinsky's attorney and the special prosecutor over an immunity agreement that would protect Lewinsky if she told her story.

As the week progressed, saturation coverage of the scandal continued with unprecedented ferocity. Speculation was widespread that Clinton's days in office were numbered; some commentators spoke openly of impeachment. Against this backdrop, Clinton met with his cabinet to assure them of his innocence, and within hours advisers who had defended Clinton during the Gennifer Flowers matter were back on television telling everyone who would listen that the president is innocent. In the wake of intense media coverage, it was a hard sell, but the Clinton team was relentless. On January 26, Clinton issued his strongest denial to date, saying "I did not have sexual relations with that woman, Ms. Lewinsky." The next morning, during an interview on *Today*, First Lady Hillary Rodham Clinton blamed the scandal on a "vast right-wing conspiracy" that was out to get the president—and the counterattack was in high gear. That evening, in a confident performance in which he did not mention the scandal, the president gave his State of the Union address to a joint session of Congress and a larger-than-usual television audience. He received high marks from reporters for his poise under pressure, and within a few days his job approval rating was at its highest mark ever. The public appeared to be saying that, despite doubts about whether Clinton was telling the truth, the press and perhaps the special prosecutor had taken the matter too far too fast. As he had done with the Flowers scandal, Clinton successfully played hardball politics and survived a political firestorm that had threatened to consume his presidency.

## High-Stakes Policymaking: NAFTA, 1993

In the period between these two scandals, President Clinton faced an entirely different set of obstacles as he attempted to move an often complex and controversial legislative agenda through Congress. One challenge he assumed during his first year was to win ratification for a free-trade pact negotiated by his predecessor that would reduce exchange and investment barriers with Mexico and Canada. The **North American Free Trade Agreement (NAFTA)** would provide for open trade among the continent's three large countries. But it required congressional approval in the United States, and it was controversial. During the presidential campaign, candidate Bill Clinton was cautious about NAFTA, saying he would support it only if Mexico acquiesced to side agreements mandating strict labor and environmental laws.

That was in 1992. The following year, Clinton as president got those side agreements and had to decide whether to move forward on the trade pact or sidestep it entirely. His decision to push for passage came in the face of opposition from both the right and left of the political spectrum. Among Democrats, organized labor strongly opposed the measure, fearing low Mexican wages would threaten American jobs—a fear shared by some conservatives. In late summer 1993, when Clinton made the decision to push NAFTA, all sides in the debate agreed that the votes needed for congressional passage were not there.

By early September, the Democratic leadership in the House had been torn apart by the measure. First, House Democratic whip David E. Bonior of Michigan, the third-ranking member of his party in the House of Representatives, defected to lead the opposition to the pact. As whip of the president's party, Bonior would typically be expected to line up votes for the measure. But organized labor is strong in Michigan, and Bonior decided to break ranks with the president.[11] Then the second-ranking House Democrat, Richard Gephardt of Missouri, joined the opposition. Add organized labor, environmental groups, and former independent presidential candidate Ross Perot, and NAFTA opposition was broad, well financed, and strong.

Perot spearheaded a media blitz to defeat the agreement that included a spate of television and radio appearances and publication of an anti-NAFTA book *Save Your Job, Save Our Country*. U.S. trade representative Mickey Kantor responded on behalf of the administration with a seventy-four-page rebuttal of his own. In a move that generated ample media coverage, President Clinton began to make deals to win votes. Backed by an unusual alliance that included members of the Republican congressional leadership, Clinton contacted representatives he felt he could persuade to discuss special arrangements. Many of these were limited to industries in members' home districts that might be affected by free trade. For instance, Representative Lewis F. Payne, Jr., a Virginia Democrat, asked for special protection for textiles in order to consider voting yes. In early October, the president agreed, although Payne remained uncommitted.

Many such exchanges would follow for the next several weeks, along with intensive lobbying by interest groups that stood to be affected by NAFTA. Florida vegetable growers pressured the administration and the Florida House delegation to restore tariffs on lettuce, peppers, squash, cucumbers, and tomatoes. The sugar industry worked to have corn sweeteners protected from Mexican imports. Lobbyists for everything from wine to bedding tried to protect their interests in the face of potential changes in trade regulations.

As interest-group representatives lobbied Congress and the president, and as the president made individual deals with members of Congress, Kantor continued to negotiate with Mexico in order to extract more favorable terms that could win over a few wavering representatives. Meanwhile, all parties waged a publicity war. During the week of October 18, the president unveiled plans for retraining workers who might lose their jobs to Mexico, provided the details of a proposed border cleanup plan, and hosted a free-trade "bazaar" in which businesses that stood to gain from NAFTA displayed their goods on the White House lawn. Opponents fought with equal vigor; on October 20, Bonior held a news conference and posed a knotty question for people to consider: "How many products that used to be made in America have we lost to Mexico?"

All the while, the legislation was working its way through Congress where it was on the "fast track" to a vote. This means Congress agreed to consider the bill without amendment within ninety days of its submission. By September 30, the first draft of NAFTA legislation had cleared the House Ways and Means Trade Subcommittee, and within a month, representatives of the full Ways and Means Committee would meet with representatives of the Senate Finance Committee to iron out differences in wording and introduce the same version of NAFTA in both houses. A final vote in the House was scheduled for November 17.

But support for NAFTA was still as tentative as opposition to the measure was strong. Consequently, in early November, Clinton made the risky choice to have Vice President Gore debate Ross Perot on CNN's "Larry King Live." Gore often appeared stiff and unconvincing on television, but the administration believed it could gain momentum by having him confront the quipster billionaire. Administration aides felt they could simultaneously make Perot the symbol of the anti-NAFTA forces and discredit him by playing on doubts many people were beginning to have about his competence and judgment.

The strategy worked. The feisty Texan indeed appeared petty and petulant to many people who watched the debate or heard commentators talk about it. Reporters remarked how Perot had been "gored" by his own quick temper, a judgment reinforced by postdebate opinion polls. If the debate itself did not change many minds, it did provide political cover to uneasy representatives who wanted to vote for NAFTA.

After more intensive White House lobbying and last-minute concessions from Mexico, NAFTA was approved by the House of Representatives on November 17 by a 234–200 vote. It passed the Senate three days later, 61–38.

## Conclusion

It should be apparent from this brief overview that politics and governance concern a number of groups with a stake in the political system. The discussion of the 1992 New Hampshire primary mentioned the public (as voters, contributors, supporters, and opponents), political parties, candidates and their advisers, and the media. Each of these is a potential actor in the story that appeared in the press. Similarly, the NAFTA proposal involved the president, members of Congress, organized interest groups, the public (as constituents), and the media. The particular constellation of groups may vary, depending on whether the issue is politics or policymaking, but each group is a stakeholder in the political system, and the way we respond to how they are portrayed has the potential to shape how we view that system.

The remainder of this book will examine these portrayals and the messages they send. Several things will become apparent. We will observe how so much political coverage, particularly on television, centers on the actions, needs, and fortunes of the president, even though so many other groups and individuals are critically important to what happens. We will explore how politics is frequently portrayed as if it were a military contest—the media building on the inherently interesting nature of conflict that is so much a part of politics to the exclusion of other equally apt metaphors, such as politics as reasoned debate or politics as statecraft.

Conflict is interesting because it is divisive, and we will see how coverage tends to emphasize this element of politics as it dwells on the processes of creating legislation or getting elected rather than on the fruits or merits of these processes. In this approach, less is said on the policy positions of the presidential candidates than on their media strategies or personal histories, and there is less coverage of the merits of NAFTA than of President Clinton's political investment in winning passage.

And we will see how reporters frequently give center stage to themselves and their interests. The "inside" details of a media campaign can become headline news, as can the needs of reporters covering political figures. Although correspondents may seem to operate in a peripheral capacity relative to other political participants, we will see how it has become standard for reporters to elevate themselves above the role of supporting actor in the stories they tell. For instance, a significant portion of the coverage of the Lewinsky matter was about how journalists felt about the media's coverage of the scandal.

The ease with which reporters write themselves into their stories reflects the importance of the media to advancing the agendas of political figures. Traffic on the information superhighway runs in both directions, and presidents, members of Congress, interest-group representatives, party spokespersons, candidates—virtually every group with an interest in political outcomes—will at some point attempt to use the media to promote their objectives. To do so is not new. But for reporters to talk about what these groups are doing and how they are doing it, as they now routinely do, is to add a new, decidedly cynical twist to coverage. Such news items lay bare the more manipulative elements of power and policy struggles, providing the audience with a dubious framework for understanding all things political.

Chapter 3 will examine these items as they apply to politics at the presidential level; Chapter 4, as they apply to governance. Each chapter will consider both the composition of coverage and the meaning of politics conveyed by the media. Chapter 5 will assess the overall picture of politics conveyed to the American audience in the 1990s, revisit questions of public cynicism and distrust in light of these images, and attempt to discern what the future holds as new information technologies and emerging media outlets rewrite the rules of the political game. Although we will devote most of our attention to mainstream media because they are the news source for most Americans, we will in the end examine alternative and nascent media as possible sources of different messages about the system.

First, however, it should be noted that political coverage as we know it has pertinent antecedents. In Chapter 2, we will try to put today's political discourse in context by looking at the roots of the historical place of the media in American politics. If today's reporting is aggressive, cynical, and harsh, how was it in the past? The answer may surprise some: The particulars of coverage notwithstanding, political news as it appears today has evolved over the course of the twentieth century, and in some important respects it traces its roots to the formation of political parties in the early days of the republic.

# 2

·····································

# Two Hundred Years of Politics and Reporting

This is a new medium called television.
It's so powerful that it's changing the
whole media structure of the world.[1]

—Thomas Rosser Reeves, Jr.,
Eisenhower advertising strategist

To think that an old soldier should come to this.[2]

—Dwight D. Eisenhower, on acting
for campaign commercials

．．．．．．．．．．．．．．．．．．．．．．．．．．．．．．．．．．．．．．．．．．．．．．．．．．．．．．．．．．．．．．．．．．．．．．．．．．．．．．．．．．．．．．．

T eddy Roosevelt called the presidency a "bully pulpit," and he didn't even have MTV. But an analysis of the techniques Roosevelt used to massage reporters into covering his version of events will reveal striking similarities between one of the first presidents of the twentieth century and one of the last. Roosevelt and Bill Clinton, both activist presidents, saw the media as a direct link to the public for their presidential initiatives and as a forum for building a personal political following. Their techniques differ: Roosevelt was the first president to hold press conferences and the first to permit reporters to work inside the White House. Clinton held only two formal press conferences in his first eighteen months in office and once toyed with the idea of tossing the White House press corps to quarters next-door. But the intent behind their actions is remarkably comparable: to use the media to develop a national constituency for a strong presidency.

It wasn't always like this. The way political figures regard the media has changed greatly during our history. And over the course of two centuries since the ratification of the Constitution, the nature of the press itself has developed dramatically. But despite the fact that the media of today look vastly different from the media of 1800 (or 1900 or 1980), several parameters describe the emerging association between the press and politics. Understanding them should help clarify the present contours of that relationship.

1. *The press has always played a pivotal role in both politics and governance.* Over the course of time, the political rules of the game have changed and changed again. The right to vote has been extended to people who did not own property, then to nonwhites, to women, and to eighteen-year-olds. Presidential candidates have been selected by congressional caucus, then by political party conventions, then through widespread popular primaries. Political parties, once strong links between citizens and government, have gradually grown weaker. And through it all, the press has retained its prominence as a vital political medium. Although political circumstances helped determine the exact role the press would play, information dissemination has always been vital to electoral politics in the United States. Candidates quickly learned that control of news was a key to gaining power.

So it is with governance. President Thomas Jefferson relied on newspapers to promote his political agenda, and every activist president since has depended on the media in some manner to fashion a coalition for his initiatives. This has occurred despite the fact that the rules of governance have been rewritten many times since 1800. President Clinton regularly bypasses Congress and uses television talk shows to campaign for his legislative initiatives. Thirty years ago, President Lyndon B. Johnson might have held a press conference for the same purpose. Sixty years ago, President Franklin D. Roosevelt would have used radio to form a bond with the public that could be used as leverage in his dealings with Congress. And almost two hundred years ago, President Jefferson would have used newspapers to present the partisan line of the Democratic-Republicans to loyal and faithful readers.

2. *The role of the press in politics and governance has been continually redefined by technological advances.* As new media have emerged, they have been used consistently for political purposes. Today, Bill Clinton can beam his likeness via satellite or target select audiences by appearing on a cable channel; broadcast television is almost taken for granted as a political fixture. But if Clinton represents a generation of political leaders weaned on television, his predecessor, George Bush, came of age politically when the powers of the tube were being discovered. Through the 1950s and 1960s, politicians came to know the immense power of video to build and at times destroy political careers.

Earlier in the twentieth century, radio fostered a breakthrough in political communication unparalleled in its day. Citizens who had never heard a president could listen as Franklin D. Roosevelt metaphorically entered their homes to offer reassurance during depression and war. Prior to radio, politicians relied on newspapers, which flourished for a long period in the latter half of the nineteenth century as a consequence of technological advances in printing.

With each advance, political figures could reach a broader audience in a more intimate and sophisticated way that introduced new opportunities and posed new problems to those who would lead. In this regard, the story of politics in America is the story of the emergence of new communication technologies.

3. *National political reporting has always been intertwined with the presidency.* In the early days of the republic, when newspapers were partisan organs of political parties, presidents could readily control what was printed and directly shape the public debate. By the turn of the century, as newspapers shed their political affiliations and became competitive for readers, they found the president (in no small part because of the careful stroking of Teddy Roosevelt) to be an irresistible source of news. This remains the case today; turn on any network evening newscast and count the number of stories about the president relative to stories about senators, representatives, governors, or mayors. The chief executive is still chief newsmaker.

Interestingly, this dominant presidential role has encompassed periods in our history in which Congress was the predominant national institution. The president has always been the favorite of the press, for as the only singular officeholder in government, he is a natural magnet for coverage and best positioned to present a focused message. If we think of eras in our history in terms of presidential administrations, such as the "Reagan years" or the "Eisenhower period," it is due in no small part to the presidential focus of the news.

This emphasis is reflected in the following historical account of media politics. We will consider select examples from the past, with particular consideration of the post-1950 period, in order to place the current state of media politics in a meaningful context. Names like Roosevelt, Eisenhower, Kennedy, Nixon, and Reagan will assume prominence in this discussion because each man contributed significantly to changes in the relationship between reporters and national political figures. The chronology is not meant to be exhaustive, however, for numerous episodes and individuals contributed to the evolution of the role of the press in politics.

Neither is this focus meant to suggest that presidents were the only players in the process. To that end, the discussion will consider key moments in congressional use of the mass media and a successful case of interest-group lobbying in 1994 that was magnified by the media beyond its intended proportions. Along with the presidency, Congress and interest groups will be salient factors in our subsequent discussion of media politics.

# From Party Press to Penny Press

## *The Party Press: Attack Politics as Mainstream Journalism*

The present tendency for reporters to rake political figures over the coals has deep roots in American history. The earliest newspapers were partisan publications, owned and maintained by political parties and operating as vehicles to disseminate the party line. Although contemporary media might attempt to approach all political figures equally (if not with equal amounts of hostility) in the effort to maintain objectivity, operators of the party press blatantly attacked their political opponents. Objectivity was unnecessary, indeed undesirable, because the mission of the paper was to maintain a political base among its readers and unify supporters against the opposition.

The reason for this approach to journalism was economic. During the earliest part of the nineteenth century, newspapers were circumscribed in their ability to publish in large numbers. Because technology was limited, printing costs were high, and there were relatively few urban areas outside of Boston, New York, Philadelphia, and Baltimore to support a wide readership. But if supporting the cost of publication through subscriptions was impractical, turning to patrons to cover costs was not (Rubin, 1981).

Political groups proved to be a natural locus of ownership because the access newspapers provided to the citizenry was a critical resource to emerging political parties. As early as the 1790s, emerging Federalist and Republican camps found the linkages newspapers could create with the public to be central to political organization.

Although these party organs initially attempted to win support through reasoned argument, by the time Thomas Jefferson became president, reporting took on the character of personal attacks and blatant partisanship. For instance, this passage from the Washington, D.C., *Daily National Intelligencer* was typical of nonobjective election coverage in 1820:

> Monday next is the period fixed by law for the people of Maryland to choose Electors of President and Vice President of the United States. So well conducted and so happily administered has been the government of the Union under the auspices of the present Chief Magistrate, that the united voice of the nation again calls him to preside at the helm of state. . . . Truly enviable must be the feelings of the venerable [President] Monroe in being assured that out of the millions who are free to choose, scarcely a solitary demagogue is found to say *nay* to his re-election (November 7, 1820).

Today, with political parties no longer in control of the press, such obvious partisanship would be considered grossly inappropriate. But one tendency remains the same: The way the party press covered politics appealed to the lowest common denominator among readers, even if it also served the useful purposes of intensifying political differences and mobilizing an emerging electorate in a relatively new political order.

## The Penny Press: Selling Sex and Scandal

Sex sells newspapers in 1999. It sold newspapers in 1899. Once the party press gave way to the private commercial press, the nature of the lowest-common-denominator appeal began to convert to the sort of coverage that could attract a mass audience.

Technological and economic changes helped bring on the transformation. By the 1830s, technology was making possible the production of goods for a mass market. This created the need for promotion and advertising. At the same time, technological changes were beginning to make publishing newspapers easier and less expensive, a trend that would continue throughout the nineteenth century with the development of the telegraph in 1844 (making it feasible for newspapers to support a far-flung network of reporters), linotype in the 1880s, and lower paper costs toward the end of the century. The result was a natural marriage of advertiser and newspaper, geared for a mass audience (Exoo, 1994; Rubin, 1981).

Lower production costs and the onset of advertising revenue made newspapers suddenly affordable. In 1833, the *New York Sun* debuted for the meager sum of one penny per issue (down from the six-cent cover price of party newspapers) and found that the way to sell papers to a large readership was to give the people what they wanted—which as media scholar Doris Graber puts it was "breezy crime and sex stories" (Graber, 1993: p. 118). Other papers followed. In the 1880s, newspapers owned by Joseph Pulitzer and William Randolph Hearst institutionalized what became known as **yellow journalism,** which featured lurid details of sensational stories complete with screaming headlines and eye-catching illustrations. The technique caught on: Between 1883 and 1886, Pulitzer's *New York World* increased its circulation from 15,000 to over 250,000 (Exoo, 1994).

What did not sell, however, was partisan politics. Reaching a mass audience meant toning down the party line so as not to restrict circulation to Republicans or Democrats. Consequently, the party newspapers that had been the media mainstay during the early part of the nineteenth century declined in the wake of the new environment. By the early twentieth century, objectivity would emerge as a desired goal for coverage and as a standard of excellent reporting among journalists. The revolution from party press to neutral press would be complete.

This meant, however, that politicians who wished to use the media to promote their political and policy agendas needed to redefine their relationship to the press. Presidents like Thomas Jefferson and Andrew Jackson could easily control the message that appeared in print because the medium was an arm of their party organization. With this capacity undermined by the penny press, politicians needed to find more subtle ways to convince reporters to tell the story they wanted told.

As the century progressed and technological advances provided political leaders with advanced tools for agenda control, the strategies they employed became increasingly sophisticated. Over time, this put politicians at odds with reporters, who came to resent efforts they felt were designed to manipulate and undermine them. By the end of the twentieth century, the relationship between politicians and the press had turned 180 degrees from what it had been at the dawn of the republic. Once lords of the message, politicians had become opponents and at times enemies of a press corps they felt often stood in the way of their efforts to achieve political and policy goals.

## Candidates or Products?

In the political arena, the change was gradual. Those who followed the 1952 presidential contest probably thought it looked a lot like the election of 1948: Candidates appeared at rallies, made radio addresses, took "whistle-stop" train tours through the country, and made fairly traditional speeches about American values. Those continuities notwithstanding, the way campaigns were conducted changed irrevocably that year. For the first time, television was a strategic factor in the conduct of the campaign, and advertising agencies were employed to craft an image of a national candidate to sell to the electorate. Even though television as a medium was in its infancy and not yet the national force it would become, the way politicians reached voters changed forever after 1952. The dawn of the modern hi-tech campaign was at hand.

## BBD&O Likes Ike

The candidates that year were as different as their attitudes toward the fledgling television medium. Governor Adlai Stevenson of Illinois, the Democrats' standard-bearer, was a meticulous, intellectual man who held television in low esteem and eschewed its use for political ends. He campaigned on the force of reason and argument, making eloquent appeals to the voter's intellect that frequently failed to establish a fervent, visceral connection. General Dwight D. Eisenhower, the Republican nominee, was not only a World War II hero at a time when America was engaged in an unpopular war in Korea but also a nonpolitician when political corruption preoccupied many voters. If he lacked Stevenson's feel for words, he more than compensated for this shortcoming with his down-to-earth demeanor and his reputation for strength and honesty. He was also willing, unlike Stevenson, to turn these qualities over to an advertising agency to maximize their impact on the electorate.

The advertising firm of Batton, Barton, Durstine, and Osborn (BBD&O) was hired by the Eisenhower campaign to develop a theme for the candidate that could play well on television and to implement that theme in a television marketing strategy that would present the voters with a picture of Ike they could enthusiastically embrace. BBD&O's image makers decided to promote Ike-as-war-hero, to enhance the picture of a likable Ike that many voters already had in their heads. They purchased television time in thirty-minute blocks in which they presented carefully scripted Eisenhower appearances that played to the emotional connection voters had to the candidate: Eisenhower surrounded by cheering crowds, Eisenhower flanked by his adoring, supportive wife Mamie, Eisenhower in a sea of American flags. Formal stump speeches, until then the mainstay of presidential campaigns, were minimized, in part because Eisenhower's delivery was stilted, in part because they insufficiently communicated the candidate's magnetism. In their place, the audience was cued to recall why they indeed liked Ike.

While BBD&O repackaged Eisenhower for the media, the Ted Bates agency planned and produced for the campaign the first television commercials ever used in a national political contest. The commercials were the brainchild of ad-man Thomas Rosser Reeves, Jr., whose previous contributions included not-so-subtle commercials for toothpaste, soap, and aspirin (including an Anacin ad that depicted a hammer pounding away inside someone's head). His approach to marketing Eisenhower was just as blunt: Catch the attention of the viewer, and make the message simple (Halberstam, 1993).

The Eisenhower ads opened with a still picture of the candidate to the left of the words "Eisenhower Answers America." They cut to footage of an "ordinary" American asking the general a question like "Mr. Eisenhower, are we going to have to fight another war?" or "The Democrats have made mistakes, but aren't their intentions good?" Eisenhower then appeared on screen in a tight shot, filmed from the chest up, in which he answered the public's questions with retorts like "Well, if the driver of your school bus runs into a truck, hits a lamppost, drives into a ditch, you don't say his intentions are good; you get a new bus driver" (Diamond and Bates, 1988: p. 58).

To maximize the effect of the candidate answering real voters, Reeves refrained from using actors to ask the questions and instead recruited tourists to Radio City Music Hall in New York who looked to advertising agents like mainstream Americans. But their questions were scripted for them—based on marketing research into the concerns preoccupying real voters—and written on cue cards. In fact, Eisenhower's "answers" to their questions had already been filmed at a daylong session with the candidate in a New York studio. But when the final product aired, it gave the impression Reeves desired: the sincere, caring candidate responding in earnest to the queries of ordinary people. It wasn't sophisticated, even by the standards of the day, but it was effective (Diamond and Bates, 1988).

For his part, Stevenson used television grudgingly and ineffectively and condemned the Eisenhower campaign for trying to market its way to the White House. He did not watch television, and he did not think much of it. When he did appear in the medium, it was in a format more suited to radio: Stevenson's aides purchased eighteen half-hour slots at the same time period each Tuesday and Thursday evening in which they aired speeches by the candidate or his supporters. They had intended to create a loyal following for Stevenson's regularly scheduled program, much as an audience at that time might have followed a radio or television serial. But the audience never emerged, owing in part to Stevenson's refusal to air produced material. So disdainful was the candidate of the medium that he would regularly disregard time cues, causing the network to pull the plug on the governor in mid-sentence with no more than the terse announcement that the time allotted to his program had expired (Halberstam, 1993; Diamond and Bates, 1988).

Given the political dynamics of the 1952 race, it is probable that Eisenhower would have defeated Stevenson even without an effective television campaign. For all the manipulation inherent in the Republican effort, BBD&O played to preexisting impressions of the candidate without trying to create a patently false version of Eisenhower for mass consumption. But the blatant attempt to use television to enhance the image of a presidential candidate marked a watershed in American politics; the strategy raised questions about whether the president should be a commodity that could be packaged like soap. In years to come, the questions would only grow more complicated as the medium became more sophisticated. But 1952 was the year the genie was released from the bottle. The Eisenhower campaign made it clear how the medium could be intentionally manipulated for political ends.

## Checkers

One important sidebar to the 1952 Republican campaign was a televised address by Eisenhower's vice-presidential running mate, a young senator named Richard Nixon, orchestrated by Nixon to save his place on the ticket. In September of that year, the *New York Post* ran a story to the effect that Nixon was receiving money from a dubious fund established by wealthy supporters. Eisenhower, never a strong admirer of Nixon and cautious not to appear to condone wrongdoing, left it to his running mate to clear his own name. The vacuum created by Eisenhower's distance had the effect of permitting the story to mushroom in the press and made it inevitable that Nixon would have to handle the allegation himself.

Nixon decided to confront the charges in a live televised address to the nation. On September 23, 1952, he gave a virtuoso performance that demonstrated the overwhelming personal power of a visual message and proved television's value as a tool for moving millions of people. Nixon had been coached on how to play to the camera, and he came to the speech with an intrinsic sense of the power of television, so it was not surprising that his speech was effective. With his wife Pat serving as a prop, Nixon revealed the painful details of his impoverished past—complete with a reference to how his wife, in lieu of mink, owned "a respectable Republican cloth coat" (Halberstam, 1993: p. 240). In a passage that would forever tag the address as the "Checkers" speech, Nixon spoke emotionally of his dog:

> We did get something, a gift, after the nomination. A man down in Texas heard Pat on the radio mention the fact that our two youngsters would like to have a dog, and believe it or not, the day before we left on this campaign trip we got a message from

Union Station in Baltimore, saying they had a package for us. We went down to get it. You know what it was? It was a little cocker spaniel dog, in a crate that he had sent all the way from Texas—black and white, spotted, and our little girl Tricia, the six-year-old, named it Checkers. And you know, the kids, like all kids, loved the dog, and I just want to say this right now, that regardless of what they say about it, we are going to keep it (Diamond and Bates, 1988: p. 72).

The material was hokey and painfully personal, but it was effective. Nixon had asked viewers to send telegrams supporting his place on the ticket. About one million did. It was an unprecedented demonstration of the power of television to move massive numbers of people, on a scale far more profound than what any political organization could do. And it was a harbinger of things to come as subsequent presidential candidates—including Nixon himself—turned primarily to the small screen to mobilize public opinion.

## Kennedy's Television Mystique

By 1960, 87 percent of American homes had television, and political figures had perfected the techniques first employed by the Eisenhower ad agencies eight years earlier. John F. Kennedy was the first politician to capitalize on the potential political payoffs afforded by the picture tube, parlaying his boyish good looks and easy wit into celebrity status. When Kennedy announced his candidacy for president in January 1960, he was a relatively junior senator with a limited legislative record. But over the course of that year, he skillfully employed television to develop a presidential mystique. He embodied what has become a commonplace phrase: He was the first "telegenic" candidate and president.

Kennedy the candidate had the capacity and the foresight to use television to project an image of leadership and strength tempered by compassion and accessibility. He hired a speech professional to lead him in voice exercises, and he paid meticulous attention to how television could exaggerate his mannerisms. Cultivating the right image was a self-conscious endeavor. Before his acceptance speech at the Democratic National Convention, his brother and campaign manager Robert Kennedy had reserved seats surrounding the speaker's podium filled with people off the streets, so that the picture on television would reveal a large enthusiastic crowd greeting the newly anointed nominee. In a move that anticipated Bill Clinton's saxophone-playing appearance on Arsenio Hall's show thirty-two years later, Kennedy made a visit to the "Tonight Show" in June 1960 to chat with host Jack Paar. The effect was to neutralize the potential handicap of youth by generating the appearance of Kennedy as a fresh, energetic leader (Watson, 1990).

Through the camera lens, the somber Richard M. Nixon seems a drab alternative to the vigorous John F. Kennedy. Photo courtesy UPI/Bettmann.

Perhaps the most remembered element of the Kennedy media campaign was the series of four fall debates with Richard Nixon, the Republican nominee. Although today the public has come to expect its presidential candidates to engage in a series of televised debates, there was no precedent for such a format in 1960. The idea originated with the television networks, all three of which invited the two candidates to confront each other on the air. Both candidates accepted—Kennedy because he stood to gain in stature from appearing on the same stage with his opponent, the incumbent vice president; Nixon because he was concerned about the impression he might create if he appeared to back down from a fight.

Although Nixon, the Checkers-speech veteran, had more experience with television, Kennedy understood the medium more profoundly. Kennedy's performance helped elevate the young senator to presidential status and deflate Nixon's claim to be the only qualified candidate. The reasons were largely visceral. On television, Kennedy appeared to be vigorous and in control, particularly in contrast to Nixon, whose eyes would dart and whose upper lip would sweat profusely under the hot studio lights. Furthermore, during the first debate Nixon suffered from the image-dampening effects of weight loss caused by a recent illness;

Kennedy, in contrast, benefited from having a suntan and from having crafty aides who understood the sharp impression a blue shirt could create on the black-and-white screen. Differences between the two men were far less apparent to those who heard the debate on radio, where Nixon's strong tactical debating skills garnered high marks from listeners. But on television, where nonverbal communication mattered more than words, Kennedy looked not only to be Nixon's peer but also to be the healthier, more fit—more qualified—candidate (Watson, 1990; Schlesinger, 1965).

## The New Nixon

Eight years later it would be different. Back from a brief period of self-imposed political exile following his whisker-thin defeat in 1960, Richard Nixon again won the presidential nomination of the Republican party, pledging to himself to learn from the mistakes of his earlier losing effort. The lesson he learned was about image manipulation. He recognized that the primary goal of Kennedy's media campaign had been to sell people the *idea* that a relatively junior senator could be presidential. He realized that he needed to do the same thing if he were to prevail, and that it would be a hard sell. In 1968 the idea of *President* Nixon was odious to many who thought of him as shady and untrustworthy, the shifty-eyed character of the Kennedy debates and the "Checkers" speech. Because he had been around so long, Nixon was an established political figure, and a lot of people had a negative impression of him. Quite possibly, the Nixon that people knew could not win a presidential election. Nixon's solution to this dilemma was to reinvent himself, to create a "New Nixon" people would be willing to send to the Oval Office.

To do this, Nixon and his advisers embarked on what at the time was an unprecedented image management campaign. In a strategy that extended far beyond Kennedy's attempt to craft a persona of skillfulness and caring, Richard Nixon sought to reinvent himself by carefully controlling every element of his latest run for president. By this time, it was understood that to run for president required a full-scale public relations effort, and both Nixon and his Democratic opponent, Vice President Hubert H. Humphrey, secured the assistance of advertising agencies. What was shocking and controversial in 1952 had become routine. But the Nixon public relations effort deviated from the Eisenhower initiative not simply in its level of sophistication, which was higher, but in the degree of management Nixon exercised over fabricating an image of the candidate that differed from existing public perceptions (Chester et al., 1969).

Eisenhower had been a trusted and respected figure even before BBD&O got hold of him. Nixon never enjoyed that level of respect. So he set out to convince the electorate that the things they may not have trusted about him no longer applied. The "New Nixon" would be likable, beyond reproach, and ready to assume leadership. This task required a well-orchestrated sales job. Two factors central to the effort were constant regulation of the message emanating from the campaign and careful staging so that the candidate seemed warm and sincere on television, though there were many indications that he wasn't like that in real life. According to one close campaign observer, the real Nixon was "grumpy, cold, and aloof" (McGinniss, 1969: p. 31).

But such discrepancies were not to get in the way of the sales effort. After trumpeting his intention not to "barricade myself into a television studio and make this an antiseptic campaign" (McGinniss, 1969: p. 62), Nixon proceeded to do essentially that. Television studios afforded him utmost control, and he appeared in ten regional broadcasts that all followed the same format: A panel of seven carefully selected people (eight, his aides thought, would appear too big) would interact with the candidate in front of an audience of Nixon enthusiasts. The objective was to create a subliminal effect on the audience: to get the viewer to identify with Nixon as he faced what appeared to be an uncertain or even hostile crowd composed of people who at face value did not look like Nixon supporters, then to project an air of warmth and likability as he proceeded to win over that crowd by virtue of his intellect and humanity.

Of course, the gathering was not hostile, and no element of the broadcast was left to chance. Racial and religious balance would be achieved by including on the panel one African American (two or more were assumed to be too risky), a Jew in certain markets, a Mexican American in Texas. The set would place Nixon in the center for dramatic effect but was small enough to create an intimate feeling. Makeup was carefully employed to avoid a repeat of the sweating problem Nixon experienced in his 1960 television appearances. And the press—truly a hostile force—was kept out of the studio (McGinniss, 1969).

The Nixon campaign understood that the essence of television sales is the creation of a positive experience for the viewer, which could be achieved through careful programming. This philosophy was reflected in the way the campaign controlled and coordinated all facets of image production from commercials to public appearances. It was well stated in a memo drafted during the campaign by staff member William Gavin:

It's the emotion that gets across, the posture, the sense of involvement and concern. [President] Johnson can never achieve this; he doesn't project, or if he does it's with a calculated intensity. *It's got to appear non-calculated.* . . . To the T.V. oriented, it's doubly important that we make them *like* the candidate. They're emotional, unstructured, uncompartmented, direct; there's got to be a straight communication that doesn't get wound through the linear translations of logic (McGinniss, 1969: pp. 187–188, first emphasis added).

Nixon won sufficient votes to squeak past Humphrey in one of the closest elections in American history. In so doing, he established a new standard for message control in presidential campaigns. Although the deviation between produced and private persona would not always be as stark, every subsequent successful presidential candidate would rely on the sort of packaging that sold the "New Nixon" to a reluctant public.

## Leaders or News Managers?

As mass media advertising began its slow infiltration of the political sphere, elected leaders were discovering they could employ similar sales techniques in governance. Just as the emergence of mass communication technologies gave politicians new avenues for reaching and persuading large numbers of voters, so too they gave representatives the parallel ability to set and advance policy agendas. In governance as in politics, the change was gradual at first and revolved around the development of television. As politicians, particularly presidents, aggressively seized new opportunities for agenda control offered by skillful use of the mass media, effective governing—like effective campaigning—became defined by communicating a carefully controlled message to a large audience.

### FDR: News Management Model for Contemporary Presidents

In several respects, the model for contemporary governance may be found in the pre-television presidency of Franklin D. Roosevelt. Teddy Roosevelt was the first president to market his agenda by promoting the presidency as a focal point for national news; FDR elevated **news management** to an art form. Determined to control what the press said about him and his administration, FDR endeared himself to reporters and manipulated the relatively new technology of radio to construct the public persona of a caring president.

When FDR assumed the presidency in 1933, Americans still got their news primarily from print media. Roosevelt therefore knew the importance of establishing good relations with the newspaper reporters whose words filled the columns of the major dailies. In many respects, his method for developing those ties with reporters was simple: Satisfy their needs. Roosevelt cultivated reporters by taking an interest in their professional concerns and by permitting them unprecedented personal access. He made himself available to reporters at times convenient for them, such as at breakfasts and lunches, and in sharp contrast to predecessors Warren Harding, Calvin Coolidge, and Herbert Hoover, he made sure that news items flowed constantly from his administration. Blessed with a flair for public relations and an understanding of what would look good on the front page, Roosevelt was able to explain often complex material in an easy, straightforward manner that made it simple to report the story. Even when he avoided answering questions, Roosevelt maintained an open feeling with the press corps through a high level of personal accessibility that included inviting all reporters to at least one state function per year (Winfield, 1990; White, 1979).

If this access gave reporters the constant source of news they craved, so too did it give Roosevelt control over the news agenda. Every time FDR provided grist for the next day's headlines, he was helping to determine how his presidency would be covered. Although not all coverage was sympathetic, FDR's understanding of what made headlines permitted him to regulate much of the information published about his administration. And his ability to win over reporters personally made it easier for him to get the press to relay that information in the fashion he wished. The press corps had little desire to play by different rules because they naturally benefited from Roosevelt's approach.

As he managed traditional forms of news dissemination to his benefit, FDR also had an instinct for how important emerging technology could be to building an image of a strong, caring president. He was the first president to realize that electronic media provided an unprecedented forum for message control and image building. Radio had been around for well over a decade before FDR took office; his immediate predecessor Herbert Hoover made twenty-seven radio addresses in 1930. But Hoover was an ineffective speaker who didn't understand the personal nature of a medium that families would listen to together in their living rooms (Winfield, 1990).

Roosevelt knew the potential, and during his initial days in office he delivered the first of what CBS radio bureau chief Harry Butcher dubbed "fireside chats" for their intimate, informal nature—as if the president were in the living room sitting by a roaring fire with the listener. The phrase stuck, and FDR became known for these talks, which were replete with colloquial phrases like "my friend" that were delivered in a sincere manner to a depression-era public clamoring for reassurance.

For instance, in his first fireside chat, on March 12, 1933, Roosevelt began with a straightforward, direct pronouncement about the crisis of widespread bank failures: "I want to talk for a few minutes with the people of the United States about banking" (Burns, 1956: p. 168). He proceeded to do just that: to break with the tradition of long-winded presidential orations and to speak for about twenty min-

FDR's strategic use of radio, particularly his "fireside chats," gave millions of listeners an unprecedented sense of access to the presidency. Photo courtesy the Bettmann Archive.

utes in simple, comforting phrases that people could understand. So popular were the fireside chats that people would write to the White House asking for more—but FDR, ever aware of the dangers of diminishing his stature through overexposure, gave only four in his first year and only a handful more after that.

Similarly, FDR was the first president to realize the importance of repeating the same message in different media for maximum effect. During the Great Depression of the 1930s, people could also get their news at cinemas via newsreels, brief movie versions of the news of the day that would accompany feature films. Forerunners of television news, these "talking newspapers" provided many people with their first pictures of distant places and famous people, including the president. FDR made it a practice to have some of his radio addresses filmed for newsreel use, repeating highlights that he wanted seen in the theaters for the newsreel cameras after he finished his broadcasts. These filmed messages had the effect of reinforcing what the audience had heard on the radio and permitting the White House further control of the message that reached the public (Winfield, 1990).

Roosevelt was able to communicate his message so effectively in part because of the climate of the times in which he served. He assumed the presidency during the depths of the Great Depression, when the public was looking for the kind of reassurance the fireside chats could offer, and when reporters were poised to embrace an administration that, unlike its predecessors, would give them a place at government's table. Nonetheless, Roosevelt would not have been able to effect his media strategy so completely had he not recognized how to massage the press and public or had he lacked the appropriate communication skills. In maintaining effective control of the news agenda for large portions of his unprecedented twelve years in office, Franklin Roosevelt set the standard by which subsequent presidents measured their news management efforts, just as he led the way in demonstrating how to incorporate new media into governance.

## Kefauver and the Mob: The First Television Miniseries

Future generations of political officials would find in television a medium they could exploit in much the same manner Roosevelt used radio and newsreels, only to a larger audience and to a more profound extent. But it would take some time. In 1951, television was still something of a novelty, even though it was beginning to find its way into many American homes. In New York City, for instance, slightly more than half the residences had television sets—up sharply from 29 percent the previous year—making it the first metropolitan area on earth where a majority of homes were wired for video (Halberstam, 1993). The fledgling television networks had already connected large portions of the East and Midwest to the communications system that would eventually transmit television shows across the country. Although programming was still scarce and amateurish by today's standards, the new medium was poised to make its mark on society and politics in a manner few could have predicted.

One of the first political incidents to qualify as a televised media event was a 1951 Senate hearing held to investigate the relationship between organized crime and urban politicians associated with **political machines**, a label applied for the organized, corrupt manner in which they stifled political opposition by providing assistance to voters in exchange for political support. On the face of it, Senate hearings seemed an unlikely subject for a television spectacle; after all, they tended to be dry and routine. But the novelty of television afforded the viewing audience an unprecedented glance at the halls of power. As it turned out, the subject of these hearings made for excellent theater.

One by one, underworld figures took a seat in front of the Senate committee and testified about their business ventures and their relationships with urban political leaders. In a manner that would foreshadow every televised political event to come, what they said was far less consequential than how they looked on the flickering screen. In a word, they looked like criminals; their manner of dress and coarse speech conjured up images of gangsters in the minds of viewers across the country who, because of television, were privileged to participate as passive observers to the hearings.

The most dramatic moment came on March 13 during testimony by Frank Costello, the reputed leader of the New York underworld. Unwilling to show his face on television, Costello agreed to have the cameras train their gaze on his hands. The results, according to author David Halberstam, were "devastating":

> Those hands relentlessly reflected Costello's tension and guilt: hands drumming on the table; hands gripping a water glass, fingers tightly clenched; hands tearing paper into little shreds; hands sweating—all the while accompanied by the words of the committee's relentless pursuit. . . . Some 70 percent of New York City television sets were on, which gave the hearings twice the ratings achieved by the World Series during the previous fall. People in the other cities hooked up were also mesmerized. The newspapers wrote stories about husbands coming back to find the housework unfinished, their wives glued to the television set and wanting to talk only about the inner workings of the mob. In New York, Con Ed had to add an extra generator to supply the power for all the television sets (Halberstam, 1993: p. 192).

If the hearings themselves made surprisingly good television, the chair of the committee conducting the investigation made an unlikely television star. Estes Kefauver was a junior senator from Tennessee, a nondescript individual who came across as awkward and ill at ease in front of audiences. But on television, this hapless quality gave Kefauver the appearance of the ordinary man fighting crime and corruption, good clearly juxtaposed against evil.

Whereas television made Frank Costello appear guilty by hand-wringing, it made Kefauver into a celebrity. In a manner familiar to today's viewing audience, the televised hearings catapulted Kefauver to a level of fame unprecedented for a freshman senator. He appeared on magazine covers and game shows, wrote a best-selling book about his crime investigation, was offered a small part in a Humphrey Bogart movie, and despite widespread evidence that he was something of a philanderer, was voted father of the year. He made a credible run for the presidency the following year and eventually cashiered his fame into the Democratic party's vice-presidential nomination on a losing ticket with Adlai Stevenson in 1956 (Halberstam, 1993).

This type of instant celebrity is now so commonplace that it may be difficult to imagine just how unusual it was in 1951. The American public had learned for the first time just how powerful the visual medium could be as a public relations and public policy tool. Even though large portions of the country were unable to receive the broadcast, the Kefauver hearings had a national impact on the substance of the crime investigation and on the political fortunes of the senator who conducted it. The power of pictures as a political device had for the first time become evident. Months before the Eisenhower campaign would demonstrate how television could be intentionally manipulated to market a candidate, the Kefauver hearings illustrated how the medium could have unanticipated effects on policymaking by making a formal investigation into a public event and turning anonymity into glamour and fame.

## "See It Now": Murrow and McCarthy

Nevertheless, in the Kefauver hearings television was still an accidental player, a passive messenger whose power surprised even the senator who benefited politically. In contrast, an on-air confrontation three years later between a senator named Joseph McCarthy and a newsman named Edward R. Murrow underscored the ability of a reporter to use the power of the new medium to change the course of political events.

McCarthy was a relatively obscure junior Republican senator from Wisconsin in 1950 when he started making unsubstantiated accusations about Communists holding positions in the U.S. State Department. His charges resonated in the icy Cold War atmosphere of the postwar world, propelling McCarthy to great notoriety and launching a witch-hunt that lasted for years. McCarthy's anti-Communist crusade touched all levels of public life: government, academia, the entertainment industry, the military. His tactics were always the same: to slander individuals with innuendo, to imply—without evidence—present or past involvement in activities or organizations sympathetic to communism. As he ruined reputations, his influence grew, and as his influence grew, public figures lived in fear that they would be named next. To speak out against McCarthy was to risk one's livelihood, and in this intimidating climate the senator could operate in a vacuum without vigorous press scrutiny or vocal public opposition.

In this atmosphere, a CBS news reporter named Edward R. Murrow decided to use television to confront the senator. The decision constituted an enormous risk. The network knew that if McCarthy was not diminished by Murrow's challenge, the senator would go after its corporate sponsors, potentially putting CBS out of business. And as a television network, CBS was licensed by the **Federal Communications Commission** (**FCC**), the regulatory arm of the federal government with jurisdiction over broadcasting. The FCC had the power not to renew CBS's license when it expired. Fearing this consequence, CBS had previously buckled to pressure and required its employees to sign oaths of loyalty pledging that they were not Communists. But Murrow was a journalist of unquestioned reputation and was given latitude to act by a reluctant network that might simply have stifled any of its other reporters (Kendrick, 1969).

The forum for Murrow's challenge to McCarthy was a program called "See It Now," which in its own right represented a revolution in television news. When it premiered in fall 1951, Murrow, seated in a television control room, would point to a monitor bearing a picture of the Atlantic Ocean, then to a monitor next to it bearing a picture of the Pacific. As the images on the monitors shifted, respectively, to the Brooklyn and Golden Gate Bridges, the viewing audience was treated for the first time in history to simultaneous pictures of both coasts. The metaphor was clear: Television had at its disposal the unprecedented capacity to unify a vast nation (Schoenbrun, 1989).

In that spirit, Murrow worked carefully to find the appropriate time and format to take on McCarthy. The date of the broadcast was to be March 9, 1954. Murrow decided to let McCarthy do much of the talking and through this approach allow the senator to use his own words to expose himself as a demagogue. It was a masterful stroke, designed perfectly for television. Filmed footage of McCarthy ranting unfounded accusations ran contrapuntally to Murrow's calm statements of fact; the result was to make the senator look like a fool. Despite a CBS prohibition against on-air editorializing, Murrow closed his broadcast with these words:

> We will not walk in fear, one of another. We will not be driven by fear into an age of unreason, if we dig deep into our own history and our doctrine and remember that we are not descended from fearful men. Not from men who feared to write, to speak, to associate, and to defend causes that were, for the moment, unpopular. This is no time for men who oppose Senator McCarthy's methods to keep silent. . . . There is no way for a citizen of a Republic to abdicate his responsibility (Kendrick, 1969: p. 53).

It was the beginning of the end for McCarthy. Telegrams to CBS ran ten to one in support of Murrow, and McCarthy's rating in the Gallup poll the following week dropped substantially. CBS invited McCarthy to respond on the air (which he did, giving an enraged performance in which he accused Murrow of every imaginable disloyalty), but it was too late. The broadcast gave others who suffered McCarthy in silence the cover to speak out, for the senator's shield of invincibility had been pierced. After "See It Now," McCarthy was forever on the defensive.

Murrow personally disliked the broadcast and brooded about his performance. But perhaps his most profound reaction to the encounter was about the power of television that had been demonstrated that night in 1954, one that would ring true in the years to come. "You and I know that I'm the guy in the white hat," he told a colleague. "But what could a guy in a black hat do if he had the power of this medium in his hand as I did?" (Schoenbrun, 1969: p. 76).

## Kennedy in Office

Over forty years later, Murrow's musing remains a key question for our time. The period between the McCarthy broadcast and the second Clinton administration is marked by the increased use of sophisticated communication techniques by political leaders bent on mobilizing public opinion in support of policy agendas, and journalists determined to report the news in an increasingly aggressive fashion. This fact alone is not problematic. But the process has generated troublesome by-products that call into question the balance between power and accountability. Even if the medium has not been exploited by someone with clearly evil intentions, as Murrow feared, it has tempted ambitious people to milk its considerable advantages; this has fueled a rift between officials and journalists that over time has had dubious consequences for democracy.

As was often the case in twentieth-century media politics, change happened slowly. John F. Kennedy was the first president to make a distinction between the media and the press—a key distinction that allowed him great latitude to set the public agenda with minimum interference from hard questions asked by reporters, and one that would serve as the core media strategy for future administrations. For Kennedy the president, it was a natural extension of the campaign techniques he had used to win the White House: He became the first president to incorporate a political media strategy into governance.

An important component of that effort was the televised press conference, which worked as the debates had to provide Kennedy with a heavily watched forum for evoking favorable audience response to his leadership. Building upon FDR's use of press conferences to win the loyalty of White House reporters a generation earlier, Kennedy held encounters with the media to woo the press and to enhance his public image. He was the first president to conduct live televised press conferences, and he did so on a regular basis.

Like the carefully crafted picture of large crowds cheering his convention acceptance speech, press conferences offered Kennedy a forum he could control. He came well rehearsed, with a clear sense of the message he wanted to leave his audience. And he never lost sight of the fact that he was speaking to the camera even as he faced the reporters: The true audience for these performances was in homes across the country (Kern et al., 1983; Watson, 1990).

This approach made Kennedy the first president to distinguish between television as a communications vehicle and the reporters who traditionally transmitted the message, and to bypass the latter as he used the former. It was a conscious strategy. As he once remarked to a journalist, "When we don't have to go through you bastards we can really get our story to the American people" (Watson, 1990: p. 76).

In the process of building his image, Kennedy and television inflated the importance of the presidency as a singular source of hope and progress, generating bloated performance expectations inconsistent with the constitutional design of the presidency as but one branch of a slow-moving system. This perspective would continue after Kennedy's death. American politics would revolve even more tightly around the president as the chief executive continued to dominate the medium that was fast becoming the primary source of public information. But for subsequent presidents, television's intimacy would not be as kind as it had been to Kennedy. As his successor discovered, the same camera that was capable of granting political life could undermine policy and drive a president from office.

## War and Scandal

The power of television over the course of public policy had never been more evident than during the Vietnam War. By the mid-1960s, network news had come of age, attracting larger audiences to a more refined product. CBS and NBC began offering thirty-minute evening news programs in 1963; ABC followed two years later. These developments coincided with the escalation of American involvement in Southeast Asia, and the conflict made it inevitable that pictures from the battlefield would be seen in millions of American homes for the first time in history.

As in the past, technological improvements brought changes in coverage. Lightweight camera equipment enabled television news crews to follow troops into the field. Jet air travel made it possible to transport footage from Vietnam to the United States within a day of filming. If these developments seem primitive when contrasted with the speed-of-light reports that emanated from Baghdad during the 1991 Persian Gulf War, consider that bulky cameras and brief fifteen-minute news reports had frustrated television coverage of the Korean War a mere fifteen years earlier (Wyatt, 1993; Hallin, 1986).

As an entertainment medium, television places a premium on the dramatic and the visual, and the Vietnam War proved to be an immense source of arresting pictures. But it would be misleading to suggest that television news saturated the airwaves with bloody battlefield footage during the early years of the war. Although Vietnam had become a regular story by 1965, the typical broadcast emphasized relatively bland statements by public officials. By one count, less than one-fourth of television stories prior to 1968 included combat footage, and only a similar percentage included pictures of the dead or wounded; particularly graphic footage was often edited as a matter of network policy. It would be more accurate to say that television had access to such pictures, and that their presence, no matter how limited, on the fledgling evening news programs marked a dramatic departure from all previous war reporting (Hallin, 1986; Braestrup, 1983).

As the war intensified, so did television and newspaper war coverage. The turning point was the North Vietnamese attack known as the Tet Offensive of 1968. As fighting engulfed the capital city of Saigon, cameras were well situated to record it. Some of the images were brutal. This report aired on ABC in February 1968.

A terrified dog breaks from his hiding place and searches for safety but doesn't really know which way to run. People are running, too, heading for the open country to get away from death in the streets. Some had once fled to Saigon for safety. This Vietcong terrorist was captured; the troops lead him to the front of the An Quang Pagoda, headquarters for the militant Buddhist faction, and there Brig. Gen. Nguyen Ngoc Loan, the embarrassed and angry man in charge of police and defending the capital, executes him (Braestrup, 1983: p. 351).

That same month, venerable CBS anchorman Walter Cronkite went to Saigon and issued a report that some see as the turning point in the Vietnam War. In it, Cronkite offered his assessment that the best conclusion the United States could hope for in "the bloody experience of Vietnam" was "stalemate":

On the off chance that military and political analysts are right, in the next few months we must test the enemy's intentions, in case this is indeed his last big gasp before negotiations. But it is increasingly clear to this reporter that the only rational way out then will be to negotiate, not as victors, but as honorable people who lived up to their pledge to defend democracy, and did the best they could (Braestrup, 1983: p. 134).

It was an editorial observation from a highly influential CBS correspondent, reminiscent of what Murrow had said about McCarthy 14 years before. And it was just as powerful. Having seen this report, President Johnson is said to have remarked "It's all over"—a phrase that could apply to the war and to his political career, as he shortly decided not to seek reelection. Throughout his term, Johnson had tried feverishly to control the way Vietnam played in the press, sending surrogates to appear on television talk programs to espouse the administration line and pressuring publishers to try to get them to ease up on what he believed was negative coverage. Sensing he had failed, Johnson frequently castigated the press for what he felt was a disservice to the American public and a personal affront to the presidency. "Unfortunately," Johnson told a sympathetic audience in 1967, "a student carrying a sign or a protester wearing a beard, or an attention-seeker burning a draft card in front of a camera can get more attention—and more billing—

Television emerged as a powerful force in international policymaking when it personalized the Vietnam War for the U.S. audience. Photo courtesy UPI/Bettmann Newsphotos.

than all 10,000 volunteers enlisting in the military in a single week" (Turner, 1985: p. 217).[3] It was an admission of defeat for Johnson, but also a harbinger of things to come for the relationship between politicians and reporters. In the coming years, far worse would be said about and by journalists on and off the air.

Although the reasons for the Vietnam tragedy are many and complex, Vietnam was the first large-scale policy event in which the role of television became a hotly debated subject, and it marked the first time a president felt it necessary to take on the networks for what he believed was irresponsible reporting. Much of the conflict between press and president centered, as usual, on control. It raised important questions about the appropriate role of the press, including how much of the war television should be allowed to show, how much deference should be given to the administration, and how much the administration could do to stop coverage it didn't like.

These questions would echo through the final years of the administration of Johnson's successor. Having waged a successful campaign of what at the time was unprecedented image control, Richard Nixon depended on tightfisted information techniques to direct what the public would learn about his administration. He instituted a hierarchical staff structure that regulated the flow of information between president and subordinates and jealously guarded against news leaks to the press. In response, reporters assumed a vigilant posture toward Nixon (Sanders, 1990).

In 1972, a burglary was reported at the Democratic National Committee headquarters in Washington's Watergate Hotel. Most reporters initially regarded the event as a minor story and gave it little coverage. The *Washington Post* assigned two local reporters, Bob Woodward and Carl Bernstein, to pursue the matter. Through **investigative reporting** efforts that would subsequently become the model for a generation of reporters, Woodward and Bernstein battled reluctant sources and a recalcitrant White House to trace the break-in to the Nixon administration. Once this connection was established, reporters from other media joined the hunt. Determined to control the story, Nixon repeatedly denied involvement in the break-in as he engaged in efforts to conceal his participation from the press (Chester et al., 1973).

Quite possibly, the extent of the president's role in the Watergate affair might never have been known had not Nixon, obsessed with posterity, secretly tape-recorded his Oval Office conversations. Some recordings implicated him in the cover-up effort. When those tapes became public in 1974, Nixon was forced to resign the presidency in the wake of a series of gripping, nationally televised congressional hearings on the president's role in Watergate and, subsequently, on motions for impeachment.

It is probable that Nixon's ability to manipulate information and his willingness to surround himself with others similarly inclined to such control hastened his downfall, just as they had enabled his election. Watergate festered in an atmosphere of secrecy reminiscent of the antiseptic television studio that candidate Nixon publicly disdained but privately embraced. It was exposed because of the aggressive efforts of print reporters committed to investigative journalism.

Their work was acclaimed by other journalists as a paragon of vigorous reporting and was offered as justification for an unfettered, aggressive press. Without doubt, the determination and courage of those reporters who risked their livelihoods to expose a corrupt administration did a great service for the public and the constitutional process. Their methods were appropriate to the time and place. But it didn't stop there: They were about to become the standard against which future reporters would measure their work, even those not faced with crises of Watergate's magnitude. After a decade of official deception, war, and scandal, relations between politicians and reporters were about to deteriorate. No longer would journalists give officials the benefit of the doubt or assume their political or policy motives were pure, as they might have in the past. In subsequent years, the operating assumption would be that politicians were not to be trusted, and the good journalist was one who could expose the wicked truth lurking beneath their public statements.

For their part, politicians gave reporters many reasons to believe this. Watergate did not keep future presidents from applying the visceral lessons of the Kennedy, Johnson, and Nixon administrations. Far from it; Jimmy Carter, who intentionally played on his cool, casual television persona to remind viewers of John F. Kennedy, was advised by his strategists to cultivate both the press and a "Kennedy smile" (Schram, 1977; Stroud, 1977). When the former actor Ronald Reagan entered the White House, image and message manipulation were elevated to a science.

## Reagan: Hitting the Mark

Like Nixon before him, Ronald Reagan ran a well-orchestrated, tightly controlled campaign for president that effectively managed the message the candidate wanted disseminated: that Ronald Reagan was a compassionate sort who could be trusted with the presidency. Much as Nixon used the media to re-create himself, Reagan used his acting skills to persuade the electorate to rethink his past reputation as a fast-shooting cowboy who was too conservative for mainstream America.

For Reagan, the object of the game was not simply to project an appearance; it was to dominate the news agenda so as to control the direction of politics and policy. This objective was systematically pursued, often with stunning success, by a team of assistants who built around the president a public relations apparatus of unprecedented proportions. Their guiding assumption was that the more the White

House could control how its agenda was covered, the more they could neutralize their political opposition. As observer Mark Hertsgaard notes, the effort originated with a group of assistants labeled "killers" by NBC anchorman Tom Brokaw:

> The "killers" primarily responsible for generating positive press coverage of Reagan were Michael Deaver and David Gergen, and if they did not exactly get away with murder, they came pretty close. Deaver, Gergen and their colleagues effectively rewrote the rules of presidential image-making. On the basis of a sophisticated analysis of the American news media—how it worked, which buttons to push when, what techniques had and had not worked for previous administrations—they introduced a new model for packaging the nation's top politician and using the press to sell him to the American public. Their objective was not simply to tame the press but to transform it into an unwitting mouthpiece of the government (Hertsgaard, 1988: p. 5).

• • •

To achieve this goal, they coordinated the information emanating from the White House. Aides gathered to start every day by determining what they wanted coverage to look like on the evening news. Having arrived at a theme for the day, they would illustrate it with events that played to television's hunger for interesting pictures; the procedure ensured that network coverage would play the story as they presented it.

Everything was scripted by White House assistants, including the backdrops, lighting, and camera angles used for presidential appearances. Deaver acted as something of a stage manager to the president, envisioning the way Reagan appearances might play on the evening news, then acting to turn that vision into reality. Central to the effort, of course, was Reagan, the actor-turned-politician dubbed the "great communicator" for his ability to deliver his lines with ease and aplomb. His Hollywood training gave him the advantage of being able to sense how to deliver speeches with maximum impact, how to play to the television cameras, how to stand so as to "hit the mark" placed by the director for the best angle or the most striking background effect. Not inconsequentially, Reagan's acting history also made it easy for him to take direction from his media gurus, and this ensured that staged events would come off without a hitch. To the extent that television had assumed such a critical political role by 1980, it was perhaps appropriate and maybe inevitable that the electoral process would reward someone who had already mastered the medium (Maltese, 1992; Hertsgaard, 1988).

Reagan's team was so successful in its efforts to dominate the agenda by controlling the media that Reagan came to be known as the "Teflon president" because he was rarely viewed negatively by large numbers of people, even during times when his job performance ratings were low. Consequently, he also became the model for subsequent media efforts. As we will see in the next two chapters, President Clinton employed some of the Reagan techniques, going so far as to invite Republican David Gergen to cross party lines and join his administration as a key media adviser.

The task of handling media is difficult. If anything, the challenge involved in controlling information is even more complicated today than it was in the 1980s, given the proliferation and development of information technology. Whereas the Reagan administration had to contend with only three television networks, contemporary politicians also have to worry about control of their message on CNN with its real-time news dissemination capability, not to mention MTV news, talk radio, the Internet, and many other communications outlets. If these provide officials with new ways of spreading the word, so too do they impose new logistical concerns and greater risk of losing control of the message, which is to say greater impetus to clamp down more tightly on information.

## Congress—Live

During the Reagan years, the full force of the electronic revolution came to the legislative branch. After decades of rejecting broadcast equipment on the floor of Congress, the House of Representatives began permitting live coverage of general debate on March 19, 1979.[4] Members did so with trepidation. Unlike the presidents of the late twentieth century who embraced the possibilities for agenda control offered by the new technology, Congress was a reluctant partner. As a deliberative branch, Congress is slow, cumbersome, and decentralized. Members feared that television would paint an unflattering picture of representatives who often speak to a virtually empty chamber or occasionally fall asleep during deliberation. Television pictures could not capture the effort of members in committee or behind closed doors, where real progress on legislation typically occurs.

Proposals to televise congressional debate date back to the late 1940s, but members consistently rejected them. Coverage of extraordinary events like the Kefauver hearings and congressional investigation of Watergate remained the exception. However, in 1970, the House agreed to permit broadcast coverage of committee hearings under tightly defined rules. Television had become a mainstay in American life and could no longer be ignored; by the end of the decade, House members agreed to permit live telecasts from the House floor under a system that gave them control over the placement and operation of cameras. Approval of the measure came because members decided it would be better to permit controlled broadcasts than face the prospect of yielding control of the camera to television networks, which might be more inclined to show the often empty seats.

Whereas presidents attempted to control coverage through the context and content of their messages, Congress was a bit more blunt. Initially, cameras could focus only on that part of the House floor containing the rostrum where the Speaker of the House sits and the tables for the majority and minority leadership. Pictures of the seats housing the Congress at large were not permitted. Even so, the House soon developed a loyal audience. By the end of 1980, C-SPAN, the Cable Satellite Public Affairs Network, was providing House debate to over 1,000 cable systems nationwide reaching over 7 million households.

As interest in House proceedings increased, the Senate remained apprehensive, in the words of Republican leader Robert Dole, of having to "catch up with the twentieth century." Efforts to introduce television in the Senate were scuttled by filibusters in 1981, 1982, and 1984. Precisely because of the effectiveness of techniques like the filibuster, whereby a minority of forty-one senators can kill legislative proposals by refusing to permit them to come to a vote, many senators were reluctant to permit the public to view the often arcane ways of their chamber. With its long history as a closed body where delay tactics are part of doing business, the Senate did not lend itself naturally to the camera's glare. As one opponent of coverage put it, Senate debate "is not pretty."

But by 1986, senators faced a different and equally troublesome problem. C-SPAN coverage of the House had become popular enough to give that chamber an unprecedented level of public visibility. Together with the Reagan message-control effort, the televised picture of national government amplified the president and the House at the expense of the Senate. Ultimately, the fear of becoming the invisible branch convinced enough senators to institute live coverage, first on an experimental basis, then as a permanent fixture. Initially, fearing an image problem when the cameras arrived, some senators pressed for rules changes that would have curtailed filibusters and long quorum calls that delayed debate. But these changes proved to be politically charged and were not approved.

By July 1986, the Senate voted to permit cameras in its chamber on a permanent basis. C-SPAN and the commercial television networks would have access to the pictures. Senators on both sides of the issue submitted that regardless of the particulars, the Senate would never again be the same place. And in some ways, this came to pass. Shortly after coverage began, a study indicated that although most of the work of the Senate continued behind closed doors, the number of floor speeches had dramatically increased. Senators, like presidents before them, began to take advantage of their newly implemented electronic platform as their institution emerged from relative obscurity.

## Harry and Louise

Like political candidates and officeholders, lobbyists seeking to influence the political process have capitalized on advances in media technology. For salient, important policy discussions, such as the 1994 congressional debate over health care reform, numerous interest groups attempted to influence the debate with newspaper, television, radio, and periodical advertisements. By one count, forty-eight organizations purchased ads in the first half of 1994 alone, before the start of the most intensive congressional debate.[5]

Media coverage sometimes confounds or exaggerates the intended effect of the lobbying effort. A case in point is the most celebrated series of ads to appear during the health care debate, which were produced by an association of small and midsize health insurance companies called the Health Insurance Association of America (HIAA). Their television commercials featured a middle-class couple named Harry and Louise casually expressing their concerns about proposed changes to the health care system. HIAA opposed a component in the Clinton health care reform package that threatened the competitive position of small insurers, and the companies created Harry and Louise as the mouthpiece for their cause. In the ads, the couple worried aloud about the growth of bureaucracy under the Clinton plan and voiced fears about possibly losing the ability to choose their health care plan.

Strategically, the Harry and Louise commercials were not intended for the public at large but were positioned to reach members of Congress who would be influential in the health care debate. HIAA never aired the commercials on national television networks, choosing instead to target CNN and select states where key legislators lived. Consequently, only a limited audience saw the commercials.

But because the Harry and Louise ads were among the first to attack the Clinton plan, they drew fire from the White House. When the president's reaction was subsequently covered by reporters, the ads began to assume a disproportionate level of prominence in media discussion of the health care debate. Harry and Louise eventually became a symbol of interest-group resistance to the Clinton plan as a whole rather than to one element of it. Press coverage made the fictional couple a mainstay of health care coverage for an audience that, for the most part, would not otherwise have known who they were. This applied even to people who might have seen the ads, in which the names "Harry" and "Louise" were rarely mentioned.

Harry and Louise could not have became icons of the budding opposition to the Clinton health plan if not for the ease with which the media latched onto the symbolism of the ad campaign. Consequently, HIAA emerged as a player in the general health care debate despite pursuing a strategy designed to influence only select legislators and, ironically, emerged as a symbol of wholesale opposition despite its expressed intention to modify but not kill health care reform. This outcome would have been unlikely in earlier periods when the media were technologically unable to reach massive audiences rapidly and when neither the press nor politicians paid as much public attention to the actions of insiders. But in the media environment of the 1990s, when symbolic events can unexpectedly attain great significance, even ad campaigns designed like Harry and Louise to put pressure on political insiders can generate unanticipated influence.

## Conclusion

By the time Reagan took office, the relationship between the presidency and the press had changed dramatically from the days when Jefferson could spread the Democratic-Republican line through a network of party papers he effectively controlled. Presidential domination of a partisan press had given way to a protracted contest between presidents and reporters in a period of ostensibly neutral journalism, in which political figures sought to manipulate the positive coverage that had once been theirs for free.

That same tension continues in contemporary media politics. Yet despite dramatic outward changes in the rules of the game, the president's objective remains the same; the desire to exercise control over the message is as prominent today as it was in 1800. If anything, as others in the political system are afforded greater visibility, the struggle for control has become more complex and widespread.

This is perhaps unsurprising, as the political system prohibits any single participant from acting alone. Presidents have always needed to persuade Congress and the public to gain support and votes, just as interest-group representatives have long practiced the art of persuasion to promote their versions of public policy. That means getting out the message and making it persuasive. But the stakes have climbed as the presidency has grown in importance over the course of the twentieth century, as individual members of Congress have gained greater exposure under the glare of the television lights, and as methods of media control have become more sophisticated.

Some of the more intense struggles involve presidents and the press. The battle waged today against the media by the Clinton White House—a battle invested with newfound vigor as the president defends himself against the Lewinsky allegations—is the latest act in a time-honored play. The Clinton operatives are not the first to regard the media as an opponent to be conquered. If they believe the battle rages more fiercely than ever, there is perhaps a dash of irony in the fact that the incumbent's place as the reigning star in the federal constellation was made possible by the enemy, the consequence of how the television camera more naturally focuses on the president than on any other political actor.

If the imagery of battle aptly describes the presidential-press relationship—we will soon learn that reporters believe it does—it should be said that we happen to live at a time of intense fighting. Years of information control have left the press in a contentious mood befitting the atmosphere that has developed. Reporters who see news management as a form of manipulation may feel the best defense is a good offense and respond to presidential actions and pronouncements with skepticism and doubt. There is evidence that presidential coverage, particularly on television, has grown more negative as news management techniques have gotten better (Smoller, 1986). Of course, press skepticism is hardly a new phenomenon. But it may have reached the point that the press appears as manipulative as the president.

Complicating matters is the recent experience by reporters with the fruits of aggressive investigative journalism. Far from being passive victims of news management, reporters have come to realize that genuine career benefits can be had from the successful digging propelled by reporter doubt. Consider the fate of Bob Woodward and Carl Bernstein, who as a result of their Watergate reporting achieved a celebrity status rarely bestowed on journalists at that time. This was not lost on a generation of journalism students, who looked at the post-Watergate press and saw excitement and glamour and possibly fame. The means to this end would be investigative reporting, preferably at high levels of government. This required an aggressive posture and skepticism of politicians, which would readily translate into pointed political coverage. The subtle professional message Woodward and Bernstein conveyed through their accomplishment was that they had prevailed professionally beyond most journalists' dreams because they had brought down a president. Whether Nixon's actions warranted this outcome could easily be forgotten when his head is viewed as a trophy.

Hence arises a chicken-and-egg question: Is the press more aggressive because politicians have become more skillful manipulators, or have politicians had to become more controlling because reporters are out for blood? The answer to this question depends in large part on whether the respondent carries press credentials or White House credentials. Reporters will readily point out how easy it is to be skeptical of a politician's motives, but this doesn't address the fact that both Theodore Roosevelt and Franklin Roosevelt effectively made reporters partners in their presidencies, or that presidential indiscretions known to reporters but hidden from the public thirty years ago would be readily covered today. White House operatives will point to post-Watergate reporter hostility as justification for manipulating information, but Watergate itself was the product of presidential control and manipulation, which included obstruction of justice.

Regardless of where it started, both the press and political figures perpetuate the trend. As we will shortly see, television coverage has evolved to the point that the medium itself has become an appropriate topic for discussion in television news. Television reporters have begun to incorporate their professional needs and concerns into their stories, particularly when they write about elections. As candidates and incumbents and their aides and operatives attempt to arrange the camera angles or get reporters to slant a story in a favorable way, journalists have come to discuss this fact with the audience, laying bare an arguably cynical process for all to see. In essence, it has become legitimate for reporters to address how they are being manipulated.

For their part, political figures continue to market themselves as if they were dental hygiene products. This approach has been a part of presidential politics at least since Eisenhower, of presidential policymaking since Kennedy, and of congressional activity since the cameras made individual members into television figures. Interest groups, as well, use the available technology to create a market for their agendas, at times simplifying the available policy choices. Their media tactics can be particularly effective for short-term political gain, especially if they are implemented by strategists who understand how to play to the intimate, personal nature of television and by telegenic politicians.

Problems arise when such techniques clash with our higher expectations of politics. Intrinsically, we know the president or a senator is not the same as a tube of toothpaste, and we could easily grow resentful at the idea of handlers and advertising agents. To have the mechanics of political salesmanship thrust upon us on a daily basis could readily raise doubts about the people who staff political institutions, even about the institutions themselves. To hear about the details of the deceit from reporters is to learn of an important element in the conduct of public affairs. But as we will see in the next two chapters, the lack of alternatives to this type of reporting leaves room for the viewer or reader to wonder whether anyone in the political process possibly could have higher motives than short-term gain. As cynical messages become the predominant theme in political coverage, it is understandable for us to wonder whether there is anything left to government besides the promise of cavity-fighting fluoride and great-tasting gel.

# 3

..................................................

# A War of Words: Coverage of Politics and the Politics of Coverage

We don't know where the facts lie, though it's fair to point out that the people attacking Clinton on the draft have told different stories at different times. . . . My point is not to judge Clinton, it is simply to say that the character of presidents and presidential candidates does matter. And when attacks are made on character, the press ought to report them. And then let the voters decide who's right and who's wrong.

—Bruce Morton,
"CBS Evening News," February 8, 1992

BRUCE MORTON'S PUBLIC ASSESSMENT of Bill Clinton's scandal-ridden campaign says more about the way reporters think about politics than about the beleaguered candidate's woes. Arguably, character does matter in presidential contests. But Morton contends that because character is important, character attacks are valid to report—even though once reported they may create the impression of guilt to the viewing audience and, truthful or not, undermine the character of those who compete for the most important political offices. It is not clear how the audience can subsequently transcend the swirl of innuendoes, half-truths, and lies that epitomize mediated character attacks and counterattacks and "decide who's right and who's wrong." Truth and falsehood tend to blend together under the general heading of impropriety and sour like milk from protracted exposure to television's lights.

Essentially, Morton does judge Clinton—and every other politician exposed to charges of impropriety—through the presupposition of credibility that drives press scrutiny of character allegations. In so doing, he betrays the media's skeptical approach to politics at the millennium's end. Scrape away the noble language about presenting the public with the facts, and there lies strong doubt about the veracity and integrity of those who wish to lead.

This has never been more apparent than during the first days of the scandal surrounding President Clinton's alleged affair with Monica Lewinsky, a story that raised the tantalizing possibility that the president would be forced from power because of a sex scandal. On a scale unmatched by even the furious New Hampshire stories of possible extramarital sex and draft evasion, reporters were quick to overlook the term *alleged* in their hunger to report a story that CNN accurately noted had "sex, drama, power and the possible loss of power—everything soap opera screenwriters would kill for" (January 26, 1998). These events—Clinton's struggle to survive scandals in which his character was at issue in the 1992 New Hampshire primary and as president in 1998—will provide the framework for our discussion of how the media, particularly television, tell the story of high-stakes politics.

Perhaps the best way to understand the perspective on politics so prevalent in the news is to begin to think about what reporters say in the broad context of political behavior. Consider the campaign setting in which Clinton's character first became a matter of press discussion. At the time, Clinton needed desperately to convince people to keep an open mind about his candidacy. This gave Bruce Morton all the reason he needed to wonder about Clinton's veracity; throughout history, the rhetoric and behavior of candidates in tight spots have provided good reason for informed suspicion. Campaigns have been occasions for partisan figures to flaunt their opponents' weaknesses and exaggerate their own virtues. Our graveyards are filled with onetime politicians who in their prime inflated the benefits of the prosperous and peaceful life that awaited their fellow citizens under their benevolent leadership. And countless times incumbents have threatened the republic with dire consequences should the electorate be so blind as to place its faith in the hands of the opposing party.

However, if elections were only opportunities for banal rhetoric, if the flaws and shortcomings of political figures were always paramount, and if the words of politicians never amounted to anything more than a cynical ploy to gain and hold power, then it is hard to imagine that our democracy would have survived for so long. Politics is about more than exposing or covering up impertinent behavior—far more than we might realize from looking at media coverage. Likewise, the promises and admonitions of candidates that reporters may suggest are empty words actually serve a healthy purpose: They mobilize the faithful and generate interest in the campaign as much as they work to win the allegiance of undecided voters and nonpartisans. And the system provides a built-in corrective against successful politicians who really are unfit for service or who default on their word: Voters can turn them out of office in the next election.

National political campaigns can be and have been about far more than just character posturing, empty promises, and manipulative efforts to win power. They are national periods of reevaluation during which the process of collective decisionmaking yields a resolution on the course of governance for the next several years. They are times for evaluating issues of popular concern, assessing the performance of the incumbent party, and evaluating the promises of challengers. They are opportunities for widespread political participation and the peaceful expression of civic desires and concerns, manifested through campaigning, petition signing, letter writing, voting, and any of the numerous activities associated with elections in a democracy.

Each of these manifestations of the political campaign could be portrayed in the media. But generally they are not. Instead, the media portray politics—particularly presidential campaigns—as quests for the brass ring in which politicians will stop at almost nothing in order to claim the greatest power prize on earth. Candidates may discuss their answers to policy problems and political parties may draft **platforms** intended as broadly defined statements of their approach to governance; the media will explain that the real motivation behind these actions is to attain power. Thousands may greet the candidates in Omaha or New York to hear them talk about nuclear disarmament or health care reform; the national press will say that the true importance of these events lies in gauging the size of each candidate's crowds as election day draws near. This one-dimensional perspective presents electoral politics in the most cynical light because it casts the behavior of all participants in terms of how the process advances the single-minded quest for victory.

When the audience consumes such coverage, it experiences the campaign in these terms. In essence, the press is determining the frame of reference—the **frame**—within which we can make sense of the disparate information emanating from election campaigns. We could compare the frame provided by media coverage with a window frame, the scene through which will vary depending upon the size, placement, and clarity of the window as well as upon where the viewer is standing while looking out. Similarly, the manner in which information is contextualized in news stories will influence how that information is understood (Tuchman, 1978; Goffman, 1974).

Frames inevitably highlight some perspectives and downplay others as they structure the way information is communicated to readers and viewers. Through the process of framing the news, reporters may unknowingly make value judgments as they define problems, identify and evaluate their causes, and offer solutions to remedy problems. For instance, during the Cold War, a prevalent news frame interpreted some foreign policy events, like uprisings in eastern states, as problematic; identified Communist "aggression" as the cause of the "problem"; and offered U.S. involvement as a solution to remedy the perceived political imbalance (Entman, 1993). A different frame might have organized the same factual information around the judgment that uprisings in other countries are internal matters in which American involvement is unnecessary, unwelcome, or unwise. We will soon explore domestic political frames that are similarly the product of decisions reporters make about what information should be salient in news stories and how it should be organized.

Frames provide news consumers with a point of departure for making sense of the political world. Without such a reference point, it would be difficult for viewers and readers to organize the massive quantities of political information available during campaigns. In this regard, it is both inevitable that the media will provide a frame of reference for the election and beneficial that they do so. But the particulars of the election-as-power-quest frame are not preordained. To the extent that reporters, editors, and producers make choices about what to cover and how to cover it, the content of election news may be understood as the product of the decisions they make over the course of covering the story or, more broadly, as the inclination of newsworkers to see only a fixed set of items as newsworthy. Journalists are not obliged to find fault with the behavior of political figures as they frequently do; they could frame election coverage in any number of ways. That they do not is a comment on how they look through the window onto the electoral world (Kellner, 1990).

Several influences can explain how politics is framed by reporters. Two of these were discussed at length in the previous chapter as contributing factors to changes in political coverage over time: technological improvements and the rise in the importance of television as a political tool. A third factor of great importance is the decline in the strength of political parties, an element that has brought commensurate changes in how presidential candidates run for office. Each factor shapes campaigns in the 1990s and influences the way reporters, producers, and editors conceptualize the political coverage available for us to consume. We will consider them as we explore the messages contained in election news.

Our discussion of how the press frames power politics will encompass coverage of several groups with a vested interest in the political system: party elites, candidates, campaign operatives, reporters, and the public. We will look first at the relative absence of political parties from the campaign story and will examine the extent to which this is attributable to the weakening of parties as political agents. We will see how the media filled the void left by the parties' decline, a shift that reduced campaigns to personal battles among partisan competitors. We will observe how the press emphasizes the contentious elements of elections at the expense of other, more sober characterizations, interpreting even substantive events such as candidate debates in terms of winners, losers, and campaign strategy. We will follow this with a look at how television reporters wrote themselves into the 1992 campaign story, even when their relevance to the plot line was dubious. We will consider how political operatives and their work are portrayed, examining coverage of Bill Clinton's handlers, who played to the fast-paced demands of television, and Ross Perot's "infomercial" campaign, which did not. And we will conclude by examining how the "average citizen" is portrayed on the small screen—and looking at evidence that what we see on television and read in print may not always be valuable to us and our responsible participation in the political process.

Each of these elements of election coverage has a parallel in the noncampaign context in which Bill Clinton had to defend his presidency in the wake of the Lewinsky scandal. The early days of that incident were covered in a fashion reminiscent of New Hampshire in 1992. Events were personalized and related as elements of a battle, in which the outcome of the drama being watched was the survival or the demise of the administration. To this end, reports emphasized the administration's strategy to confront a barrage of bad news, complete with open references to the operatives whose task it was to manage the administration's message. And there were countless stories by and about the press, stories alternately criticizing and defending coverage that even seasoned reporters recognized was often half-baked and unsubstantiated. In short, though there were no ballots or opposing candidates, the Lewinsky scandal was a campaign of sorts, one that would determine whether Bill Clinton or Al Gore would be president at the end of the day. The fact that the story was presented in the same personalized, strategy-heavy, insider fashion as a real campaign is evidence of how consistently the press imposes this frame on politics.

## Political Parties: Missing in Action

Elections are covered by a brand of journalist called **political reporters.** They tend to be drawn naturally to the competitive nature of the election, to see politics as sport or, as we shall shortly see, war. To them, the idea of competition is so obviously critical to how they understand elections that it is an unspoken article of faith that election news will follow the contest. ABC News political director Hal Bruno scoffs at the suggestion that there is any other way to cover it. To him, elections are obviously a "test of who wins and who loses":

> If you win you get the money from supporters to keep going. If you lose you run out of money. That has happened in every single presidential election since 1972: If they don't win, they don't get the money, if they don't get the money they're out of the game. If you do not cover that aspect of it while it's happening, what should you be covering? (Kerbel, 1998: p. 209)

Essentially, Bruno is relating the tacit assumption shared by political reporters that good coverage requires understanding elections as political face-offs. He is describing the direction, pitch, and size of the window that frames the election: It is a window that looks out on the **horserace** competition of which candidate is leading, which is trailing, which underdog is doing surprisingly well, which favorite is unexpectedly falling by the wayside.

For political reporters inclined to see politics as a contest, the contemporary presidential race gives them a lot to look at. It wasn't always this way, even though electoral competition has always contained a horserace element. A generation ago, the horses had riders in the form of political party leaders, or **elites,** who were largely responsible for determining presidential nominees. For many years, presidential aspirants would first hold lower office and rise through the party ranks over a period of time, often with the help or sponsorship of party leaders. The selection of a nominee resulted largely from bargaining among elites, making the race a fairly brief, largely internal party affair. This process reflected the original purpose of political parties: to moderate and integrate the many demands of its identifiers around viable candidates for office, who once elected could convert otherwise disparate interests into policy. If the elites held the means to accomplish these goals, the objective was to provide a structure, perhaps the only structure, capable of bringing together the multiple voices of a multicultural nation (Keeter and Zukin, 1983; Ranney, 1983).

But the shape and duration of the presidential horserace have changed dramatically over the past twenty-five years in a manner that has diminished the role of political parties in selecting their own nominees and exaggerated the emphasis reporters place on campaign events and the importance of media horserace coverage to the outcome of elections.

Because of changes in the rules of competition, the race for president has become longer and less dependent on appeals to leaders of the political parties than in the past. Whereas John F. Kennedy could declare his intention in January 1960 to run for president in the November election, candidates today begin active campaigning well over a year before the election. Similarly, Kennedy could compete in only a handful of state primaries in advance of the party convention, but today's candidates must endure a relentless primary marathon that forces them to hopscotch the country looking for votes among the party faithful. This means presidential hopefuls who once channeled their efforts into winning the support of the party elites now spend months, even years, making televised appeals to voters. It is no longer an exaggeration to portray the quest for the presidency as a race among competitors who battle it out week by week for the primary votes that will provide them with enough convention delegates to ensure their nomination.

As the rules of the political game shifted, television began to replace parties as the most important institutional link between the public and national political candidates, and the trend made horserace coverage more important to the outcome of the race. The reason for this shift rests as much with choices made by the parties themselves as with the discovery by candidates of the power of television as a political tool.

Until 1968, only a handful of states held primaries. Because political party elites maintained control of the presidential nominating process, it was possible for candidates to perform well with rank-and-file voters yet fail to impress party leaders, and thereby lose the nomination. This last occurred in 1968 at a Democratic convention torn by protests over the Vietnam War and civil rights and held in the shadow of the assassinations weeks before of antiwar candidate Senator Robert F. Kennedy and the Reverend Martin Luther King, Jr. To many younger partisans, Vice President Hubert H. Humphrey was an unacceptable choice for president, identified as he was with the Vietnam policies of the Johnson administration. Yet Humphrey was the choice of the party establishment, and he was nominated for president without having run in a single primary in 1968.

Thereafter, a divided Democratic party engaged in a series of reforms designed to heal the wounds of 1968 and give ordinary voters a greater voice in the selection process.[1] A commission headed by Senator George McGovern and Representative Donald Fraser became the first of several bodies established over the next twenty years to tinker with the nominating rules. The **McGovern-Fraser Commission** established a series of procedures that greatly increased the number of states to hold primaries; the move gave Democratic voters an unprecedented hand in selecting national candidates at the expense of party leadership.[2] In 1968, only seventeen states held primaries; twenty years later, that figure had increased by twenty. The reform was a major step toward decentralizing the nominating system and wresting power from party elites with the intent of handing it to rank-and-file Democrats.[3]

Party reform was supposed to produce candidates who had widespread public support. Instead, these changes had the unanticipated effect of increasing the electoral importance of television, which in turn legitimated the primary campaign as a seemingly open, democratic way to pick a president. Rather than assisting well-known, experienced candidates, the new system favored politicians who understood how to use the medium to reach large numbers of voters and create the *appearance* of public support, especially early in the race when media attention is inevitably high. Some of these candidates, such as Michael Dukakis in 1988 and Jimmy Carter in 1976, had little or no national recognition prior to their nominations. Instead, they employed a sound media strategy and a shrewd understanding of the changing electoral rules to build an instant base of support from which to run for president (Seib, 1987; Rubin, 1981; Asher, 1980).

Candidates needed a vehicle for reaching primary voters, and television became the natural choice. The primary campaign had become a marathon consisting of dozens of individual statewide contests occurring between February and June before each presidential election. Required to reach disparate blocs of voters in distant states, candidates began instituting individual media campaigns tailored to reach viewers in New Hampshire, Florida, Illinois, or wherever the primary calendar said a vote was forthcoming. Television gradually replaced parties as the main source of campaign information and as the critical political link between candidate and voter.[4]

During the same period, campaign finance reform complemented party reform and exaggerated the effects of the long primary race. The **Federal Election Campaign Act** amendments of 1974 attempted to regulate the political influence of large interest groups by limiting the size of campaign contributions to $1,000 for individuals and $5,000 for group-sponsored **political action committees (PACs),** which are established by interest groups for the purpose of fundraising. Small contributions were further encouraged through a provision that matched private contributions up to $250 with an equal amount in federal funds in exchange for a limit on how much candidates could spend overall. With their emphasis on garnering many small contributions from numerous sources, these rules changes favored candidates who proved they could win because, as Hal Bruno noted, money always flows to would-be presidents and away from apparent also-rans. And the way to demonstrate winning potential was to endure the long primary race (Peterson and Walker, 1990).

The combined effect of electoral and campaign finance reform was devastating to the party elites. With money flowing freely to candidates and candidates depending on the media to generate exposure, party leaders began to lose the influence they once held over the nominating process. No longer could a Humphrey be nominated simply with party leadership support. Now the reverse was true: Leaders had become hamstrung by the product of reform. This rare television reference to party leaders (who are as secondary to reporters as they are to candidates),[5] excerpted from a story filed by ABC correspondent Jim Wooten during the 1992 New Hampshire primary, suggests the level of their impotence: "[Democratic leaders] are worried that if Clinton is damaged goods and wins the nomination anyway, the president [Bush] could have yet another vulnerable target. But without Clinton, the Democrats could wind up with one of the other candidates who not long ago was seen as unelectable" (February 11, 1992). This portrayal of party leaders—unthinkable a generation ago—as helpless handmaidens to an undesirable outcome aptly depicts the dilemma of those who have lost the power to broker the nomination. Instead, the real power to make a candidate has shifted to the medium on which this story appeared.

Because candidates now need to build momentum in order to survive months of primaries, they require a constant infusion of media attention. Since the media will allocate their resources to interesting—that is, viable—candidates, they readily become the arbiters of who is up and who is down. If reporters interpret a primary win to be a "knockout blow" or a loss to be a "disappointing finish," future media attention will be allocated accordingly.

Judgments designed to frame the horserace for the audience thus assume critical importance for the candidates: After all, who wants to contribute money to a candidate that disappoints, and what candidate can make an effective plea for funds without visibility? Under the new rules, media coverage has become a campaign resource as important as money, for money will come only to candidates perceived to be viable—which is to say, perceived by the press to be viable. By interpreting the horserace for the audience, correspondents thus shape the contest in a subtle but critical way. The emergence of a protracted primary contest has generated more horserace coverage, and horserace coverage has became a factor in determining real winners and losers.

This is evident in the amount of attention paid by the media to campaign events over the past twenty-five years, as horserace coverage has assumed a key electoral role. Studies of the past several presidential contests repeatedly find that references to the horserace on television outpace discussion of other campaign topics, notably the candidates' positions on domestic and foreign policy issues. This is particularly so during periods of intense electoral competition, when several horses are still in the running or when the race is especially close (Kerbel, 1998; Just et al., 1996; Patterson, 1980; Robinson and Sheehan, 1983).

But the effect is not limited to television. Political scientist Thomas Patterson finds a steady increase since 1960 in the percentage of front-page stories in the *New York Times* framed in terms of the political game. During the Kennedy-Nixon contest, the *Times* devoted slightly less than half its front-page attention to matters dealing with the candidates' prospects or electoral strategies, as opposed to news regarding policy proposals or issues. Since 1976, horserace stories have outdistanced policy stories by roughly four-to-one, as the *Times* has joined television in framing politics as a story about a game (Patterson, 1993).

The *Times* is not alone among newspapers. Figure 3.1 shows the percentage of newspaper campaign stories devoted to campaign politics during the final month of each presidential campaign race between 1968 and 1980. During the Nixon-Humphrey contest, only 35 percent of newspaper stories emphasized the contest aspect of the campaign. Instead, newspapers framed the race in terms of policies and ideas with stories emphasizing foreign affairs (30 percent), social problems (22 percent), and economic policy (13 percent). Four years later, two of three newspaper stories emphasized political news or campaign events rather than substantive issues; by 1980, the figure had grown to 81 percent.

Indeed, newspapers had come around to framing the story as it appeared on television because television coverage of the horserace had assumed a central place in the presidential contest. This was evident to any observer of the 1992 Democratic primary in New Hampshire, replete as it was with quests for a viable frontrunner amid rumors of Bill Clinton's imminent demise from the fallout of personal scandal. It was evident again six years later as the press salivated over the first details of the Lewinsky affair and speculated about whether the president would be forced out of office in a matter of days. In New Hampshire, the media presented the campaign-as-horserace frame in several distinct ways as they cov-

**FIGURE 3.1**
**Newspaper Presidential Election Stories About Campaign Politics
1968–1980**

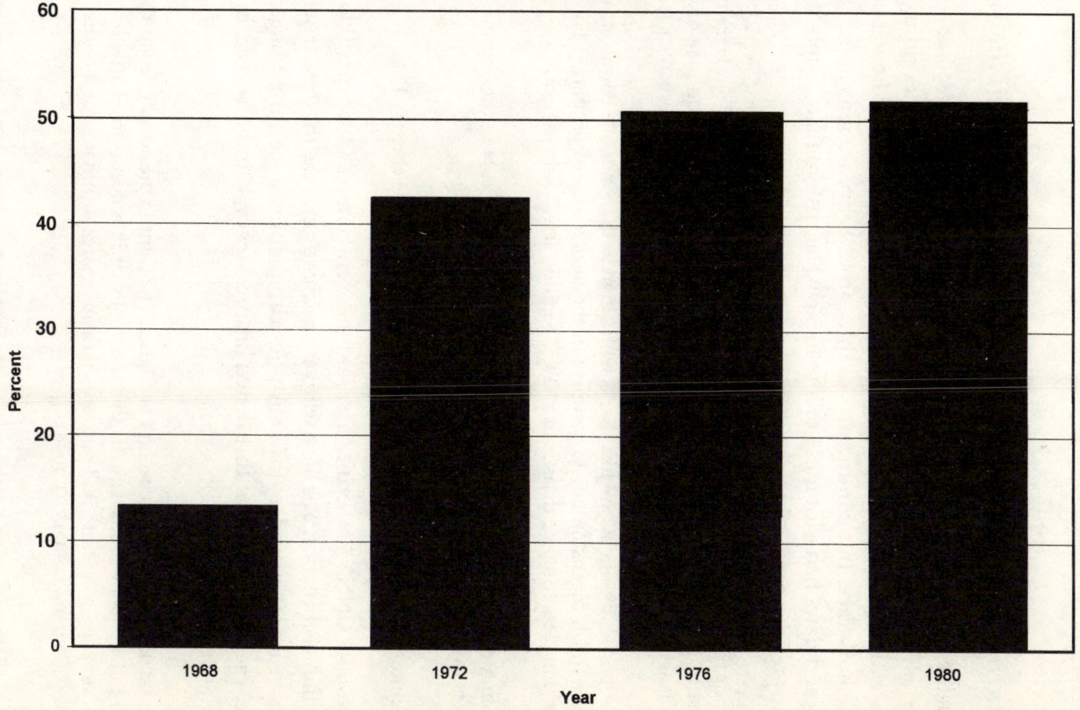

*Source:* Harold Stanley and Richard Niemi, *Vital Statistics on American Politics* (Washington, D.C.: Congressional Quarterly Press, 1988).

ered candidate posturing to win the race, strategies employed by candidates to gain advantage over their opponents, and candidate character attributes that helped or hindered the combatants' attempts to get ahead. These story elements surfaced again during the Lewinsky matter, in an extraordinary parallel to the New Hampshire race.

## Posturing to the Death: "Opening Fire" and "Blood in the Water"

Casual readers and viewers could be forgiven for mistaking horserace coverage for battlefield news. Reporters regularly mention the electoral stakes riding on candidates' actions as they interpret candidate behavior in terms of how it contributes to the horserace. But comments like these from February 1992 appear to suggest that candidates had a lot more to lose in New Hampshire than simply their dream of the presidency:

> Tsongas knew when he took the lead they'd be gunning for him. Tom Harkin was the first to open fire. . . . The stream of salvos into the Tsongas camp may only be the light artillery compared to what's ahead (CNN, "Inside Politics," February 13).

> [Clinton's] opponents are like sharks with blood in the water. . . . For most, a second-place finish means money to compete in the next round of primaries. For Clinton, anything less could be disastrous (NBC, "Nightly News," February 14).

> [Clinton] will slowly bleed to death, die of a thousand cuts in the summer and fall (*Newsweek*, February 10).

> [Clinton] appeared to be fighting for his life (*Newsweek*, February 17).

No wonder CNN's Catherine Crier said the New Hampshire primary "looms larger than life" (February 11), as life itself was apparently at stake for the participants.

Six years later, under different political circumstances, the imagery was the same. Facing charges that threatened his presidency, Clinton was again portrayed fighting for his life:

> The stakes in this battle couldn't be higher. The Clinton presidency versus the powerful independent counsel. . . . Is this the final step in a death-grip battle between Bill Clinton and Mr. Starr? Will only one of them emerge in a matter of months standing? (ABC, "20/20," January 23, 1998).

> Beneath the din of accusations, it is clear that the two determined combatants—Clinton and Kenneth Starr, the independent counsel—are preparing for what may be a long, hard engagement (*New York Times*, January 30).

Get ready for a long war. . . . Clinton and his aides have been at legal war with independent counsel Kenneth Starr for more than three years (*Los Angeles Times*, January 29).

Battlefield imagery flows naturally from the conceptualization of politics as blood sport offered by political reporters who love the action. More than a convenient metaphor, this rendering of the campaign can serve to justify reporting that emphasizes unseemly and distasteful behavior: After all, if death rather than simple political defeat is on the line, would we not expect politicians to engage in the most outrageous acts—and would not the media be remiss to avoid covering them? The practice of emphasizing cutthroat campaign behavior and questioning the motives of politicians is excusable and understandable when viewed from a horserace-as-mortal-combat frame, even if it may seem out of context to those in the audience who do not equate political victory with physical survival.

If the horserace is a war, then it is a television war, fought on television and on television's terms. The media, of course, will be the first to let the audience know this. Crier's 1992 CNN piece continued with an account of things Bill Clinton planned to do, purportedly to enhance his horserace momentum in New Hampshire. Both involved television: staging "two thirty-minute call-in shows and a tough-talk ad" (CNN, "Inside Politics," February 11). Coverage of the Lewinsky matter emphasized similar media techniques: The first lady appearing on NBC's "Today" program and ABC's "Good Morning America" to deflect criticism from her husband to his right-wing critics; the president addressing friendly crowds in thriving midwestern towns in order to generate sympathetic television pictures of a popular chief executive in control of his administration.

As in New Hampshire, the point was to generate momentum, in this case for the idea that Clinton could still govern. For instance, as the 1998 State of the Union Address approached, reporters speculated on whether the president could seize the moment and take the offensive politically. "[Congressional Democrats] felt they were on a roll, that [Clinton] had an agenda that they liked and they were ready to go with it," reported Cokie Roberts on the eve of the speech. "And now, they think it is going to be hard for him to push it, hard for people to listen, hard to get the momentum going and . . . they think that the Republicans will take advantage of a weakened President to attack them and attack them in the coming election" (ABC, "World News Tonight," January 26, 1998).

Other coverage emphasized benchmark items journalists use to assess horserace status, reporting internal considerations such as how much the New Hampshire candidates had spent on their advertising and assessments of how the candidates were doing in opinion polls.[6] This perspective was neither limited to network television nor unnoticed by other media: The author of this 1992 *Wash-*

*ington Post* story watched enough local television to be able to report, "For now, [local New Hampshire] anchors Tom Griffith and Cathy Burnham are more important than Dan Rather and Peter Jennings. . . . Horserace stories dominate local TV, with stations trumpeting polls that show a surge by . . . Tsongas" (February 12). Polls guided coverage of the Lewinsky story as well. By the end of January, with Clinton's job approval rating on the upswing, the *New York Times* was reading poll results when it wondered, "How long will this crisis drag on?":

> Just days ago, traumatized White House officials said their own polls suggested a sinking president. Prominent Democrats casually used the words "impeachment" and "resignation." The central question inside and outside Washington seemed to be, How much longer can President Clinton hang on? But now, polls show that Clinton's job approval ratings are rising (January 30).

In the political war, strength in the polls is akin to physical survival, and slippage in the polls or—worse—finishing below press-generated poll expectations is like suffering a mortal wound. So politicians are portrayed in all media as rational actors doing whatever it takes to stave off death. It is therefore easy for reporters to interpret actions of candidates in terms of the struggle they must endure, to find in their every behavior a move designed to enhance their horserace status. Given a clearly identifiable battle, such as a candidate debate, reporters will readily employ the language of competition to interpret the event for the audience.

This focus was obvious in New Hampshire following the Democrats' February 16 debate. Universally, coverage sought to determine who had "won" and who had "lost," who looked "more presidential" (a media standard for winning) and who "disappointed." The criteria applied to these judgments were cosmetic, not substantive. Candidates were evaluated on how they appeared on television or on the impression made by what they said rather than on the content of their arguments. Clinton "behaved as if he was the leader of the group," whereas Brown "continued to be the campaign's gadfly," according to *New York Newsday;* Kerrey "got off several of the best lines of the night" in the opinion of the Knight-Ridder newspapers (February 17).

But in this instance, a firm judgment of winners and losers was hard to make. Multiple candidates were involved, and as NBC's Lisa Myers interpreted it, "there were no big moments, no mistakes"—the things reporters would seize on to make horserace assessments. Consequently, coverage emphasized why there were no clear winners, predictably applying horserace criteria to understand a contest with an ambiguous outcome. Perhaps ABC's Mike Von Fremd put it best: "All along, Tsongas has refused to engage in negative campaigning, and staying above the fray may have helped make him the frontrunner, so if the message from the voters is that nice guys are going to finish first, the rest of the field wants to show they can be nice guys too, at least for the moment" (February 17).

Arguably, primary debates are a forum for comparing the candidates rather than a finite vehicle for assessing an ultimate victor. In this regard, the ambiguity that so disheartened reporters looking for a winner could be seen as not only reasonable and even appropriate but also beneficial to the ongoing decisionmaking process. But because ambiguity has no place in the horserace frame, it was equally predictable that without a clear winner or loser, the debate would be covered in terms of why things remained unresolved.

This outcome clearly frustrated reporters covering the debate, who were not bashful about passing along their dissatisfaction in their analyses of what had happened. "The mood," offered the *Washington Post,* "was so cordial that it belied the stakes." Added ABC's Von Fremd, in a reference that could more readily apply to reporters than viewers, "Anyone tuning in last night to see the gloves come off was disappointed." "The candidates," intoned *USA Today* with more than a hint of dismay, "seemed more interested in building up their own credentials than in tearing down each other" (February 17).

Curiously, the lack of a competitive resolution did not appear to bother New Hampshire residents questioned by NBC reporters as part of their postdebate coverage. Although one interviewer, Bob Kur, spoke in terms of candidate "electability" and was concerned with viewers' opinions about which candidate had helped himself the most, respondents approached the debate as additional information in the ongoing process of evaluating the contestants. Unlike reporters, they appeared interested in candidate issue positions. One voter said of Bob Kerrey, "He started out as a one-issue candidate . . . geared toward national health care. . . . [Tonight] he articulated well on other issues" (February 17).

This sort of thoughtful analysis was not featured in media coverage of the debate because issue positions get mangled by the media's horserace perspective. At times, issues are mentioned as a backdrop for how the candidates are doing competitively. An exchange between Harkin and Tsongas over the importance of manufacturing to economic growth, for instance, was framed by a major newspaper chain in terms of how the Iowa senator "looked forceful" disagreeing with his opponent (Knight-Ridder, February 17). At other times, issue discussion is simply omitted from coverage, particularly on television, for long stretches of time or is mentioned loosely in generic statements to the effect that "the candidates addressed the usual issues." Worse, substantive discussion is sometimes used as a foil for trivia. Tom Harkin's debate comparison of his urban policy with Mario Cuomo's was mentioned by a major network only to set up this horserace quip from Bob Kerrey: "Did you have to mention Cuomo? Now more people will write in his name [on the New Hampshire primary ballot]" (NBC, "Nightly News," February 17, 1992).

The most irresponsible deflection from substantive discussion occurs when reporters ignore substantive information in a story in order to maintain the horserace frame. During the campaign, it was not uncommon for reporters to say a candidate wished to talk about issues—then refuse to address the candidate's views. For instance, the *New York Daily News* reported on February 11, 1992, that Bill Clinton "spent yesterday trying—without much apparent success—to focus attention . . . on issues." Clearly, with coverage like this, no candidate could sustain a substantive message. Yet this *Daily News* piece accepts no responsibility for what it maintains is essentially a strategic failure in the Clinton campaign's effort to control the campaign dialogue. Instead, it suggests that the fault lies beyond the means of the reporter, in the horserace dynamic that requires reporters to inform readers of a candidate's intentions rather than simply to inform readers. At this juncture between horserace and strategy, substantive dialogue disappears.

## Strategy: Playing the Media Game

Coverage regularly penetrates the actions of candidates to inform readers and viewers about the maneuvers that motivate even the smallest movements of political campaigns. Political correspondents who travel with candidates and observe them during every waking hour for weeks and sometimes months become attuned to the strategies they employ in order to gain political advantage. Given the central role of coverage to political success, a candidate not surprisingly tries to get those very reporters to put the most favorable **spin,** or emphasis, on their campaign reporting by convincing them to place a positive interpretation on campaign facts.

Rather than succumb to a candidate's pressure for favorable spin, political reporters regularly report about these strategic efforts. To address candidate strategy is to remain true to the horserace frame, for reporters expect to find strategic maneuvering in the battle for coverage that is inevitable in mortal political combat. In this regard, strategic coverage is a predictable outgrowth of the horserace perspective.

But it is more than this. Because strategy entails manipulation in the pursuit of positive publicity, reporters find themselves enmeshed in the action as candidates attempt to get them to deliver the campaign line du jour. A subtle but important shift in the military perspective substitutes reporters for political opponents as the perceived enemy of the campaign. In the minds of correspondents (and often in the minds of campaign operatives), the struggle mutates to a peculiar us-against-them contest in which candidates are not to be trusted and reporters perceive themselves to be on the defensive against wily sneak attacks by guerrilla insurgents armed with irresistible words and footage.

Many reporters resent this circumstance and feel as though they need to resist the campaign in order to protect their integrity and professional autonomy. Reporters who traveled with the candidates in 1992 expressed fears of "going native" and becoming a mouthpiece for the campaign. Some fancied themselves as prisoners and worried about a "Stockholm syndrome" effect, whereby they would begin to identify with their political "captors." Still others remained hardened by what they observed to be the cynicism of campaign politics and permitted the distance this generated to inform their coverage. Said one reporter, "You come to know the candidate so well that you end up inevitably regarding him as a son-of-a-bitch" (Kerbel, 1998: p. 168). Either way, the consequence of reporter self-protection is coverage that emphasizes what motivates the candidate to act, at times to the exclusion of what the candidate does or says.

Consequently, strategic coverage is notable for what it does not say. It rarely conveys the content of a substantive political message, as reporters choose instead to emphasize the reason why the message was given. It inevitably asks the viewer to consider the motivation behind how a candidate acts, invoking the horserace frame to paint a picture of victory-hungry politicians doing what they can or what they must to achieve their goals. Some strategic coverage betrays the reporter's passive control over the agenda evident in the previous comment about Clinton's unfortunate failure to convey a substantive message. But even when it does not, strategic reporting nonetheless asks the audience to see campaign activity as a device—sometimes an unattractive device—designed to facilitate a justifiable political end.

The bevy of strategic coverage that emanated from New Hampshire during the waning days of the primary campaign there directed viewers to pay attention to a particular understanding of what the candidates were up to as they trudged around in the New England snow. Much of this reporting emphasized Bill Clinton's attempts to overcome damaging revelations about his marital and draft history. ABC's Mike Von Fremd interpreted Clinton's hectic agenda in the context of the campaign's horserace strategy: "Clinton loaded up his schedule with five events in a near-frantic attempt to reach voters and pull out of his current nosedive in the polls." Meanwhile, the *Dallas Morning News* reported what the candidate was saying in terms of his purpose in saying it: "No longer railing about Republican dirty tricks and 'cash-for-trash' journalism, [Clinton] made a studious effort to return to the forceful, upbeat message that once made him [the New Hampshire frontrunner]" (February 14). Further reference to that message was to be understood by the reader in terms of how it was being used to offset character allegations as the campaign attempted to regain its stride and achieve the one thing that matters in campaigns—victory.

Readers of the *New York Times* were told on February 10, 1992, that Clinton was employing a "stay-above-the-fray strategy that portrays him as the victim [of press coverage of his private conduct] . . . and follows these rules: ignore attacks from Democrats; play up the attacks from Republicans." That same day, the "Today" show hosted the candidate's wife, and NBC's Jamie Gangel remarked, "Wherever she goes she gets more crowds and cameras than many of the other candidates." Gangel attributed this televised observation about media coverage to "the Clinton strategy—if the American public will trust Hillary Clinton, then maybe they will trust and vote for Bill Clinton."

Six years later, there was an eerie familiarity to strategic coverage. In an echo of Gangel's 1992 observation of the would-be first lady, the *Los Angeles Times* reported:

> For Hillary Rodham Clinton, the pattern of crisis response has become almost predictable: first the silence while she struggles to guard her options and her vaunted "zone of privacy," next a tentative step to the edge of the spotlight. And for this most controversial and contradictory first lady, the culminating act is always the appearance: a gush of words, alternately combative and charming, lawyerly, arcane and homey. It comes with flawless delivery, command of detail. It is meant to disarm, to succeed. . . . It wins, for a moment at least, the admiration of many Americans (Los Angeles *Times*, January 28, 1998).

During the chaotic first days of the Lewinsky scandal, reporters were eager to tell stories about how the White House would handle the matter, just as they had framed the New Hampshire primary story in terms of Clinton's strategic maneuvering. Sam Donaldson eagerly told Hugh Downs on ABC's "20/20" about a strategic debate in the White House that culminated in the decision to do nothing. "[Clinton's] political advisors wanted him to come forward," Donaldson said, "[and] do a news conference, do an interview, make an address from the Oval Office—because they know if this story is still bubbling up [during the State of the Union Address], the public is not going to concentrate on what he has to say about Medicare and the other important problems. But lawyers say, no, you got to lie low. . . . The lawyers have won. As of tonight" (ABC, "20/20," January 23, 1998).

Other journalists explored the question of what tactics the president should use, such as whether he should impugn the character of his former intern:

> In their latest public remarks on Sunday, White House officials were careful not to attack Lewinsky. "We don't want to push her into Starr's arms," one aide said. But they clearly are mulling over strategies to pursue, depending on whether Lewinsky cooperates with Starr's investigation, and some officials suggested that her cooperation might force them to raise questions about her reliability. Quietly and subtly, some

> White House aides have already been putting out rumors that Lewinsky has an over-active imagination and may have fantasized her relationship with the president.

Consider what this coverage says about the political process. Words are attacks; spouses are props. Issue positions serve a manipulative purpose and presumably are to be discarded once that purpose has been achieved. If we are to be informed through strategic horserace coverage, it is in the ways of waging political warfare, and information that could be instructive if offered through another frame of reference becomes symbolic of the act, a mere token of battle. If such coverage is meant to serve a higher purpose, perhaps as a civics class on campaigns and elections, it should be remembered that the instructors in the media classroom are also players in the game. Reporters who convey the strategic underpinning of the campaign do so as they attempt to wrest control of events from those they cover. Their lessons to the rest of us are inevitably influenced by this condition; it is politics from the political reporter's perspective.

## Character: Personalizing Electoral Competition

A related, subtle component of this perspective is the tendency to personalize campaigns—to emphasize key individuals who substitute for more abstract processes and institutions. This is particularly true on television, where recognizable individuals (like leading candidates) serve as obvious pictorial symbols of a complex event. An otherwise complicated and protracted endeavor by the people of New Hampshire to assess the factors relevant to political discourse and make sense of numerous records, pledges, and actions is thus reduced to fairly manageable accounts of what a few people are doing, and why.

Personification becomes the journalist's shorthand for explaining the horserace by illuminating character traits that, to the writer, illustrate the campaign's pressure points. Such reporting inevitably centers on the candidates and points out how their foibles or shortcomings symbolize or cause their political situations. Late in the New Hampshire campaign, Joe Klein wrote of Bill Clinton in *New York* magazine:

> Clinton's most troubling character trait, his desire to finesse all the people all the time, seems more glaring with each new day. . . . Clinton's initial appeal was based on the sense of sureness he conveyed. . . . When he was at his best, he would challenge audiences to change. . . . After Gennifer Flowers and last week's draft stories, it may be hard to sell "personal responsibility" with any degree of credibility (February 10).

Klein pairs Clinton's optimistic nature with a destructive need to please to find the reason for his political highs and lows. Likewise, he finds in the character flaws of Clinton's opponents the reason no other frontrunner had emerged—why "it's entirely possible that the real campaign hasn't yet begun." Jerry Brown offers "industrial-strength altruism" but has not been able to convey it. Bob Kerrey and Tom Harkin "lack gravitas—or something." As for the pedantic Paul Tsongas: "It's painful to watch him. He sounds uneasy. He looks as if he's just bitten into a lemon. He appears frail."

Similarly, Susan Yoachum explained in the *San Francisco Chronicle* why Bob Kerrey's personality kept him from capitalizing on Bill Clinton's troubles in a horserace observation centered entirely on character. Yoachum asserted that Kerrey, a Vietnam veteran who served with distinction, "should benefit from [Clinton's] troubles with the draft" (February 14). The reason he did not, she contended, was because "Kerrey seems to be running against himself," displaying a "brooding" tendency that "makes him joking and affable at one juncture and almost vacant and disengaged the next."

During the Lewinsky scandal, character coverage tended to follow two speculative directions. Reporters pondered the integrity and honesty of the chief executive, musing aloud what it would mean about his fitness for office if, in fact, the allegations against him were true. And they tried to figure out why Bill Clinton would leave himself vulnerable to allegations of an extramarital affair—whether he had violated a tacit agreement with the American people that, regardless of his past, he would refrain from such activity while president—and whether he was too smart to leave behind evidence that could support the obstruction-of-justice charges. Although hardly a novelty by 1998, the president's history of being touched by serious allegations and surviving politically was itself the basis for character stories. In that regard, his personality was a natural place for character-oriented political reporters to look for news.

To be sure, some of this reporting was incidental and benign. But, at its worst, character coverage assumes a form akin to journalistic savagery, as reporters collectively latch on to a revelation of impropriety stemming from a personal shortcoming, and a crisis is born. During such times, in the words of political scientist Larry J. Sabato, "the news media, print and broadcast, go after a wounded politician like sharks in a **feeding frenzy,**" relentlessly pouncing on the scandal's principal subject (Sabato, 1991: p. 1). But if there is blood in the water, it was put there by a press corps that at the very least is guilty of tearing at a politician's self-inflicted wound.

The feeding frenzy is a form of **pack journalism,** whereby reporters from different organizations rush to cover the same story in the same manner. In the case of a feeding frenzy, they are drawn by the primal drama and excitement of a politician, injured and alone, struggling for survival. Coverage of this sort is relentless, and over the years some candidates have succumbed to the pressure, folding their campaigns and burying their political ambitions in the wake of a damaging personal story that would not die. During the 1988 presidential campaign, two Democratic hopefuls left the race when they could not surmount damaging revelations about their personal lives. Senator Joseph Biden could not transcend accusations of plagiarism while in law school and the unattributed use of another politician's words in a campaign speech. Senator Gary Hart defaulted following a well-publicized, allegedly adulterous rendezvous with a woman on a yacht named *Monkey Business*. Not surprisingly, when Gennifer Flowers told the *Star* she had had an extramarital affair with Bill Clinton, the sharks started to circle. When questions arose days later about irregularities in Clinton's draft history, the circle tightened. And six years later, when the Lewinsky allegations broke, the Flowers matter started to look like a small-time distraction.

But at the time it loomed large over coverage of the presidential election. Once the story reached the public domain, newspapers and magazines, as if in unison, featured coverage of the allegations, turning the New Hampshire primary into the Bill Clinton scandal-of-the-week club. CNN called it a "Chinese water torture," a "slow but steady drip of potentially damaging allegations" (February 6). On February 7, the day after the *Wall Street Journal* reported evidence that Clinton had intentionally avoided Vietnam service, this news dominated headlines and front-page stories across the country:

- *New York Times:* "Vietnam-Years Draft Status Becomes Issue for Clinton"
- *Washington Post:* "Clinton Disputes Draft-Evasion Suggestions"
- *Los Angeles Times:* "Did Not Duck Service, Clinton Insists as Draft Questions Arise"
- *Boston Herald:* "Draft Dispute Dogs Clinton"
- *New York Daily News:* "Draft Fuels New Fire in Bill Camp"

The *Atlanta Constitution* went so far as to acknowledge the press mind-set that produced this saturation coverage. However, in the process it lent legitimacy to the frenzy, pointing out that a respectable member of the journalistic fraternity had led the way: "For the second time in three weeks, Mr. Clinton was besieged by a press pack, but this time reporters carried copies of a *Wall Street Journal* story, not copies of a tawdry supermarket tabloid."

Such is the self-legitimating nature of character-based scandal coverage—"the *Journal* made me do it." Privately, some newsworkers admit to discomfort with, as one correspondent put it, "blasting somebody for his humanness." A television news producer said, "I know that I did not enjoy asking questions about Flowers. I prefer to ask questions of a more substantial nature than, 'Did you sleep with her?' I don't think anybody likes that. I think everyone was uncomfortable with it" (Kerbel, 1998;

p. 166). But everyone did it, which is testimony to the raw appeal of personal scandal or the reporter's competitive sense that if the *Journal* (or the *New York Post* or for some the tabloid *Star*) print it, they had better follow the pack.

Not surprisingly, once the details of a personal scandal have emerged, subsequent coverage centers on how it will influence the contest. Equally predictable is the press consensus that it will matter greatly. Any character episode salient enough to generate a media feeding frenzy is assumed to be pivotal by virtue of all the attention it commands—a verdict that readily becomes self-fulfilling the more it is repeated.

On February 6, CNN deferred judgment on the combined electoral force of the Clinton scandals but hinted that the draft story would likely have horserace implications: "Whatever its impact, this new report does come at a critical time just twelve days before the [New Hampshire] primary and amid growing concerns about Clinton's electability raised by the Gennifer Flowers flap." Four days later, that network determined that the draft story had, indeed, taken its toll. CNN's Candy Crowley estimated that the scandals had "melted some of the edge" off the Clinton campaign: "Bogged down by questions about extramarital affairs and his draft status during Vietnam, Arkansas's once comfortable frontrunner returned to New Hampshire's bitter cold Monday to what has become a dead heat." That same night, on NBC, Lisa Myers declared Clinton to be "a candidate with a cloud over his head. The next eight days will be critical," she offered, adding, "More than half the voters say they could change their minds between now and the primary." On February 12, the candidate expressed his frustration with the relentlessness of this coverage, telling ABC's Ted Koppel, "All I've been asked about [lately] . . . is a woman I didn't sleep with and a draft I didn't dodge."

Clinton's frustration had little effect on press deliberation about his potential demise. Shortly, the media began to speculate on the possible late entry of other candidates, as yet unscathed soldiers who could complete the campaign should the frontrunner die in combat. On February 14, the *Boston Globe* reported the Democratic race to be an open affair, saying "possible alternative candidates" were investigating the feasibility of a late entry. The same day, the *New York Times* fueled speculation of an expanded field by naming names: 1988 also-rans Senator Al Gore of Tennessee and Representative Richard Gephardt, the House majority leader; Texas Senator Lloyd Bentsen, the Democrats' 1988 vice-presidential nominee; Senate majority leader George Mitchell. The *Washington Post* added that "potential candidates, like others in the party are waiting" for the New Hampshire primary results "before determining what, if any steps, to take."

The press continued to report such speculation until Clinton proved he could remain viable following a second-place primary finish in the Granite State. Unlike some of his predecessors, Clinton survived the feeding frenzy unleashed by the February allegations. But they would seem like nothing in comparison to the intensity with which the press descended on the Lewinsky story, which by one measure triggered the feeding frenzy to end all feeding frenzies.

As a frame of reference for just how much the Lewinsky story consumed journalists, consider that during the week when the Flowers news surfaced, the three major networks together aired 19 stories about the scandal. Days later, during the first week of the draft dodging scandal, they aired 12 stories on the matter. By comparison, as Figure 3.2 indicates, during the first seven days of the Lewinsky drama, the networks broadcast an overwhelming 124 stories, consuming a combined 245 minutes of air time, or roughly two-thirds of the week's news hole. This rendered the Lewinsky story more saturated than even news of the death of Princess Diana, for which 103 stories were broadcast in one week.[7]

Coverage was so relentless that it was almost a grotesque parody of previous frenzies, devoid of limits and utterly lacking in balance. New technology and the enhanced speed of information dissemination fueled the frenzy. Whereas the *New York Post* was the vehicle that blessed the Flowers story with credibility, bridging the legitimacy gap between the *Star* and mainstream media, the Lewinsky scandal was born of an item in a gossipy Web site called the Drudge Report, where it was reported that *Newsweek* had researched but not published a story about the sexual allegations. Once that information was in the public domain, every mainstream news outlet rushed to beat its competitors with new information—at times covering rumor and unsubstantiated fact. It didn't take long for major media to establish their own Web pages devoted to the alleged affair.

And this time, frenzied coverage included coverage of the frenzy itself:

> It was one of those news conferences, no real news to speak of in it, but considered so important, it was carried live by every big name in news. In media lingo, it was a feeding frenzy (ABC, "Nightline," January 23, 1998).

> Within a couple of hours of Hillary Rodham Clinton's televised interview Tuesday morning, her remarks had been reported, analyzed, reacted to, recycled and boiled down to a single sound bite in the dizzying frenzy that has become the hallmark of the news coverage of the White House sex scandal (*New York Times*, January 28).

> Even the author of the book on feeding frenzies got into the discussion; said Larry J. Sabato, "It's a meltdown" (*Los Angeles Times*, January 23).

Journalists were redefining the term *frenzy* and sinking to lower levels of pack behavior than observers might have thought possible during the hectic days of

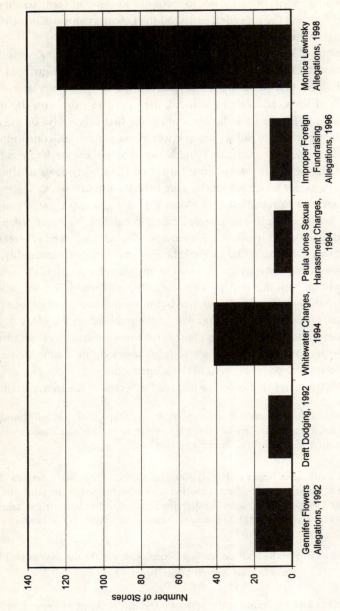

**FIGURE 3.2**

**Intensity of Coverage of Select Clinton Scandals, 1992-1998**

*Source:* Center for Media and Public Affairs

the Flowers scandal. Certainly this was in part a consequence of the speed at which information travels through cyberspace, in part a function of the fact that the story embraced sex and power in a story line that would have left editors of the penny press salivating. Perhaps the president's long history of scandalous episodes was also responsible for helping the matter explode with such force. Regardless of the causes, the result was a barrage of news more confusing than informative, more suited to overwhelming, provoking, and titillating than instructing readers and viewers.

## Reporters: The Pen as Sword

The fact that reporters referred to their own frenzied behavior in print attests to how inbred political coverage has become during the last years of the twentieth century. The tendency for reporters to treat themselves as the subjects of their own political stories, which was already apparent during coverage of the 1992 New Hampshire primary, mushroomed into an obsession once the Lewinsky allegations became public. Journalists, in earlier times passive communicators of information about political figures, have increasingly emerged from the background to talk about themselves—their political observations, their experiences covering politicians, even their thoughts about how well they cover the news. It is a dramatic departure from their traditional role as purveyors of a story about other people.

The more they speak about themselves, the less they necessarily say about the political players contesting for power, the less time and space they leave for politicians to be heard in their own words. In every respect, the story of politics becomes the story of those who cover politics. In 1968, the average network news **sound bite,** or continuous speech segment, for presidential candidates was 42.3 seconds. In better than one in five instances, networks permitted candidates to appear unedited for a minute or more. By 1988, the average candidate sound bite had shrunk to 9.8 seconds, and none were sixty seconds long (see Figure 3.3). The shortened format does not permit candidates to relate anything of meaning. Instead, their words are heavily edited to provide emphasis for a story told by reporters.

The nature of that story entails in part **self-referential coverage,** which is to say it is a story told by reporters about their own concerns. On the campaign trail, they talk about how they are treated by campaign operatives, how difficult it is to travel constantly, how the candidate they are covering says nothing particularly new as they fly together from state to state. Because traveling with a candidate can be a frustrating and alienating experience, self-referential political coverage is often decidedly cynical. Political reporters are generally hardened by life on the road

84

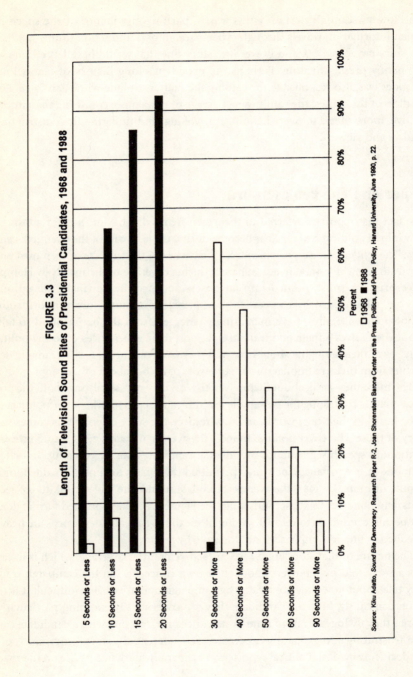

FIGURE 3.3
Length of Television Sound Bites of Presidential Candidates, 1968 and 1988

Percent
□ 1968 ■ 1988

Source: Kiku Adatto, Sound Bite Democracy, Research Paper R-2, Joan Shorenstein Barone Center on the Press, Politics, and Public Policy, Harvard University, June 1990, p. 22.

and often embattled by campaign operatives who cannot (but wish to) control the reporter's valuable airtime. As a means of fighting back, they write about their experiences in their coverage.[8]

When political reporters relate the campaign as they experience it, they tell a tale of how politicians pursuing electoral advantage struggle with the press for favorable coverage or attempt to circumvent the press to get their version of events to the public. This is essentially what Andrea Mitchell said when she reported on February 13, 1992, that "Clinton was holding his head high and blaming his troubles on the media." The comment relates the reporter's experience that winter day in New Hampshire. But it does more than this; it defines the campaign in terms of her experience. We learn of the motivation behind Clinton's words (he has trouble for which he blames the media), but we are already two steps removed from the details of that trouble and the coverage of those details to which the candidate attributes blame. In this version, the Clinton campaign becomes a hostage of the press, which has become a combatant in the political war; Andrea Mitchell is covering herself.

This sort of perspective had become so commonplace by 1998 that reporters involved in the Lewinsky story engaged in some of the most convoluted self-coverage ever to appear on television and in print. It would not be exaggerating to say there were two distinct Lewinsky stories running simultaneously: the story about whether the president had an affair and tried to cover it up, and the self-referential story about how and how well the press was covering the story about whether the president had an affair and tried to cover it up.

Newspapers and television programs were flooded with accounts of how tormented reporters were flooding newspapers and television programs with news of the scandal. These stories amounted to little more than accounts of how obsessive the Lewinsky story had become—a fact which was simply perpetuated by journalists' presence in the news:

> The news media were out in full force Wednesday throughout the nation's capital, covering one of the biggest news stories to hit this city since Watergate. . . . By noon, about 20 members of the media had assembled at the front entrance of [a] posh apartment and office complex in the hopes of obtaining footage of Lewinsky attorney William Ginsburg as they had the previous two days (Associated Press, January 29, 1998).

> Clearly, the case of Monica Lewinsky and the affair she did or did not have with the President has become an obsession. Reporters like April Ryan, whose White House reports normally focus on urban issues and minority affairs, has been filing nonstop on scandal. [Sound bite of April Ryan]: "I mean, I can't get it out fast enough. Literally while we're up in the briefings I'm getting paged to make sure I have that quote, make sure I have this, make sure I have that. So, I mean, it's something that they're, like, you know, chomping at the bit for" (ABC, "Nightline," January 23).

But the self-referential story did not stop with pieces about how reporters were spending their days or how much they were covering the scandal. It included a hefty dose of material about how ineffectively and irresponsibly they were covering the story, much of it scathingly self-critical:

> It was a moment you might expect on, say, "Geraldo," but on "Nightline"? Ted Koppel's estimable ABC late-night news program opened Thursday with the promise that viewers would learn that the "crisis in the White House" might ultimately "come down to the question of whether oral sex does or does not constitute adultery." He knew better, of course, and the opening was carefully hedged with cautions that viewers might find such a subject "inappropriate" or "an offensive issue." But it was one of those startling little moments in television when the chronic viewer senses that a wall has been breached. The sort of come-on that has served for afternoon titillation had made it into the mainstream (*New York Times*, January 25).

> What happens if the president's not guilty? After a week of coverage that in volume and tone frequently seems to presume that President Clinton did something wrong, some media experts have begun to wonder whether the reports about an alleged affair with former White House intern Monica S. Lewinsky have been lopsided and unfair. "This has been one of the most depressing chapters in American journalism," said Marvin Kalb, director of the Shorenstein Center on Press and Politics at Harvard University. Besides the steady drumbeat of rumor and sexual innuendo, there is also "a subtext of a presumption of presidential guilt" that Kalb and others feel has been an undercurrent in the reporting (*Los Angeles Times*, January 29).

Entire programs were devoted to discussions of whether the press had gone too far. Cable networks like CNN featured call-in shows where viewers could register their (often critical) judgment of how the press was doing, and journalist round-table programs where those covering the story could engage in a public defense of their work or open self-flogging (depending on the journalist) for the benefit of the home audience. Of course, none of these self-inflicted beatings did anything to improve the quality of coverage, no matter how cathartic they may have been for the participants. But they did have the odd side effect of generating even more self-referential coverage, as the public discussion of the quality of coverage itself became the subject of coverage by other reporters:

> It has hit with a vengeance: The "I-hate-myself" moment. . . . Rarely, if ever, has the examination of the coverage of a story turned into such widespread mass self-flagellation by the media, of the media, on and in the media—from Thursday's "CNN Live" program on the "Media Madness" concerning everything connected with Monica Lewinsky, to television news anchors' sheepish descriptions of their own colleagues' "feeding frenzies." Rarely have so many citizens and analysts piled on in one great outpouring of disapproval and even disgust—disgust, in particular, at how few

facts, and how much gossip and rumor, have made their way into coverage of and the accusations against President Clinton (*New York Times*, January 30).


That reporters now write themselves into the story is part of a natural progression that began when television was introduced into the political arena. By its very presence, the electronic medium changed how political figures act, altering which politicians would be successful on the national stage. For instance, without television to build a national following, a youthful candidate like John F. Kennedy could not have so swiftly won his party's nomination. Similarly, Richard Nixon, Kennedy's 1960 opponent, was a fairly good debater and might have enhanced his presidential chances in an old-fashioned debate without cameras. But the lasting memory of the Kennedy-Nixon confrontation was how the two men looked, not what they said. Television had arrived, and it had changed what mattered in politics.

Predictably, reporters took notice of the changing rules, and in short order, television became a legitimate subject for widespread analysis and discussion. As campaigns became more sophisticated in their methods of controlling the news message, much discussion centered on television tactics and strategy. Television news broadcasts had long maintained commentators, akin to print columnists, for whom such discourse was considered appropriate. But by the 1980s, this discussion had begun to filter into political reporting. Correspondents were beginning to address their own role in the shaping of political outcomes. The audience was getting a tutorial on how to run for president as told by the people who previously concentrated on the product, not the mechanics, of the effort (Adatto, 1990).

Self-referential coverage also reflects a pattern of accelerated politics made possible, perhaps inevitable, by technological advances. As we noted in Chapter 2, technology has dramatically improved reporter access to even the most remote events and accelerated the speed with which information may be transmitted great distances. Whereas Vietnam War footage was captured on film and flown thousands of miles by aircraft to be broadcast from New York, contemporary events are recorded for immediate viewing on videotape, which may be instantly broadcast nationwide or even worldwide via satellite. This has expedited the speed with which news is disseminated, heightening the professional demand for news delivered at a rapid pace while making such a presentation possible. News may now become old in a matter of hours, even minutes. If networks no longer need to wait for pictures, neither can they afford to present anything but the most updated material. This is why, in the Lewinsky case, when information couldn't move fast enough to satisfy demand, reporters found themselves relying on rumors and unsubstantiated facts.

Political coverage mirrors all reporting in its tendency to react to the technologically enhanced, fast-paced world of news by exaggerating the speed with which the story is told.[9] Shorter sound bites and compact correspondent narration are natural consequences of reporting made more concise by the demands of up-tempo presentation brought on, in part, by the ease with which videotape is gathered, edited, and broadcast. In the electoral arena, reporters are encouraged to tell their version of events rather than to permit candidates or their surrogates to drone on for a full minute or more, as was the custom when footage was less plentiful and less accessible.

Obviously, the most far-reaching effect of the new technology is felt in the rapidity of television coverage, which could not exist in its current form without portable videotape cameras and mobile satellite trucks. These are literally the lifeblood of an operation like CNN, with its two cable channels constantly beaming news worldwide. But television has also redefined news reporting for other media. Negative campaign references, we will shortly see, have sharply increased since 1980 in news magazines. And during the 1980s, the Gannett Corporation initiated the national newspaper *USA Today,* which has been derided as the journalism equivalent of fast food for its ample use of color and short articles. But the "McPaper" endures, prompting many daily newspapers to follow its lead and introduce color photographs, feature sections, and concise coverage (Exoo, 1994).

Essentially, *USA Today* is derivative of fast-forward television coverage in substance and style. Sold from vending machines that resemble television sets, it is easy to look at and to move through. Its political coverage, like all its reporting, emphasizes interesting pictures, colorful charts, and compact campaign stories. As with television, its guiding principle is be interesting and be brief.

Given this environment, political reporters gradually began to take note of the emerging importance of the media as a political tool. Over time, media strategy became a central horserace theme. Reporters began to cover campaign press relations, analyze candidates' behavior in terms of their desire for positive press, and discuss campaign efforts designed to achieve it. Concurrently, reporters started to use insider jargon once reserved for behind-the-scenes use, talking in their reports about efforts by candidates to put the best spin on their coverage, referring to campaign advertisements as **political spots,** calling campaign appearances **media events** (suggesting they are staged activities performed primarily to attract media coverage). Political reporting, always horserace-oriented, had become increasingly self-referential and cynical, as correspondents turned the cameras and microphones back on themselves.

When reporters become participants in the process they cover, they place themselves on a par with their political sparring partners, the politicians. There are no virtuous actors in the story of their battle because the tale as told has little virtue, and because it is so often told in the first person by people reporting about a system in which they play an important role. Correspondents may believe they are protecting the common good by informing the public about the manipulative ways of politicians. But by writing themselves into the story, they become trapped in a moral web, components of the dysfunctional political process they describe. In the effort to illuminate this, everyone is diminished.

## Campaign Advisers: Soldiers of Fortune

Reporters are not the only professionals they spotlight in the pictures they create. On February 12, 1992, NBC's Andrea Mitchell offered this familiar New Hampshire primary refrain: "Once again, Clinton was put on the defensive, forced to talk about his draft record instead of his economic policies." After this deceptively neutral assertion (who was forcing Clinton to talk about the draft if not Mitchell and her colleagues?), James Carville appeared on screen to level this response to the Vietnam charges: "What is the Pentagon doing in the middle of a political campaign?" Actually, one could just as readily ask: What is James Carville doing in the middle of a campaign story?

Carville, along with Paul Begala and George Stephanopoulos, was a highly placed, highly visible Clinton **campaign adviser** (or handler), the sort of person who has been operating behind the political scenes for years but who of late has taken center stage, earning a form of celebrity status once reserved for the candidate alone. Paid by the candidate to devise and implement campaign strategy, Carville, like his associates, is a campaign consultant—a "hired gun" sought for his expertise in tailoring a political message, interpreting public opinion polls, and sculpting the candidate into an electable figure. Consultants generally work either for Democrats or Republicans—although some work for both—but they are otherwise nonideological and usually leave the business of governing to the people they help elect as they move on to other campaigns.

In a departure from the past, consultants like Carville have come to occupy reporters' fields of vision as they frame the electoral campaign. On this score, what we are told about the facts of electoral competition has changed since 1972, even if the basic truths about winning and losing elections have not. A generation ago, electoral news was essentially about what the candidates were saying and how they were doing, told largely in the candidates' words. Today, it is more the story of *how* candidates are winning or losing the game. The strategic machinations critical to waging a modern campaign—employing political handlers, staging events for the media, deploying effective television commercials—have emerged from the political netherworld to take a central place in news coverage. In comparing political coverage in 1968 with its counterpart twenty years later, sociologist Kiku Adatto observed, "Like a gestalt shift, the images that once formed the background to political events—the setting and the stagecraft—now occupied the foreground" (Adatto, 1990: p. 5). With a finer lens, political reporters now view a familiar political landscape through the window and see the props and wires that hold everything up.

Officially, James Carville was Clinton's chief strategist, one of the people responsible for implementing a "rapid-response" media strategy that anticipated and answered allegations from opponents before they had a chance to linger unchallenged in the headlines. Unofficially, he also became a "talking head," one of a pool of regular sources reporters would engage for a quotable statement. Talented at turning a phrase, Carville was a natural at getting airtime and intriguing reporters with his intense, colorful demeanor. In short, Carville gave television what it wanted, and television made the backstage adviser a star.

Evidence of his celebrity status may be found in the press itself, which took Carville to be so intriguing as to make him the subject of stories. No less a popular vehicle than *People Weekly* presented a three-page spread on Carville in advance of the primary campaign's busiest weeks, gushing, "Bill Clinton's spin doctor is immersed in political alchemy—trying to turn fence sitters, naysayers and disaffected defectors into Clinton voters. Working the phones, scheduling TV spots and parsing speeches, Carville is doing what he does best—planning surprises for the opposition" (March 9). Later in the campaign, Gary Wills joined in with a biographical piece in the *New Yorker* that played on the mystique of the man political insiders called the "Ragin' Cajun" for his Louisiana background and his unusual form of self-expression: "His narrow-set eyes disappeared when his face bunched—often—in laughter or argument, or when he communed with himself as a way of divining the electorate's mood" (October 12).

Similar levels of attention were heaped on George Stephanopoulos, the thirty-one-year-old Rhodes scholar who served as Clinton's communications director. Also the subject of a *People Weekly* profile, Stephanopoulos became noted for a youthful appearance that made him look, in the magazine's words "like a college kid who has sneaked into his father's office to make long-distance phone calls" (October 26). But fueling his popularity was his visibility as the campaign's media guru. Added *People Weekly,* "It seems as if he has been on TV—becoming a fixture on the morning news shows, CNN, and 'Nightline'—almost as much as his boss." In a campaign environment built around television, such exposure is sufficient to make an assistant into a celebrity.

In the case of Carville and Stephanopoulos, their work transpired in the confines of what became known to the press, and through the press to the public at large, as the Clinton "war room." There, senior campaign staffers would monitor public opinion polls, plot strategy, and develop a coordinated message to make the campaign appear focused on television; in short, they would employ every tool possible to ensure coverage on the most favorable terms.

Like the consultants who worked there, the war room itself became something of an icon to political reporters and received its own share of coverage. In an article written several weeks prior to the general election with appropriate military imagery, Walter Shapiro of *Time* magazine observed, "Within the campaign, the power of the war room and its generals—communications director George Stephanopoulos and top strategist James Carville—has been a source of envy" (September 28).

Because of the success of the Clinton campaign, the war room received what may be the ultimate media honor: It became the subject of a movie released after the election from footage shot on location. This, in turn, served as the basis for its producers and "stars" to appear on news programs like the "Today" show to discuss the film;[10] the effect was a dizzying blend of Hollywood and television, politics and art, reality and documentary. The once-private internal mechanisms of the campaign had been publicized by the press, repackaged by Hollywood as entertainment, and elevated to pop-culture status through the media attention devoted to the celluloid war room and to the real thing. Through publicity, the media made the press manipulation of the war room legitimate. Being a hired gun became cool.

Of course, this portrayal of campaign handlers as glamorous individuals entails a certain glorification of what they do. And what they do, put simply, is control the information the rest of us receive about the candidate who employs them. By nature, this is deceptive work. Selected for their understanding of media politics, they necessarily contribute to the limited horserace perspective that has become a hallmark of partyless campaigning in the television age: Handlers know the sorts of things reporters look for and use their skills to try to work the system to their candidate's advantage. Not to do so is simply to hand the advantage to an opponent's handlers, who work the system the same way, albeit with a different spin.

However, if the publicity spotlight exposes the handlers to public awareness, it conceals the connection between their work and the dubious messages we receive about the political system. The cinema version highlights the tension and human drama of the political campaign. Television, newspaper, and magazine accounts of the cinema version entice with promises of "up-close and personal moments in the dramatic flick" (*New York Newsday,* April 8, 1993). But the glamour deflects our attention from the darker consequences of what the film portrays, much in the way the titillation derived from a feeding frenzy momentarily masks more sober and lasting messages about a political system inhabited by disappointing losers.

As the work of running for office overflows the banks of political campaigns and winning or maintaining popular support becomes a full-time presidential

job, the war room and its occupants have become a staple of media coverage. In
the years since Bill Clinton was elected president, a bevy of assistants has surfaced
in the White House—and on television—whenever the president faced a political
problem. Predictably, when the Lewinsky allegations surfaced, so once again did
the names and faces of James Carville and other political handlers—complete, as
always, with battle-related adjectives:

> Scrambling to survive the worst political crisis of his career, President Clinton has
> turned to the combat-savvy advisors who helped him escape a lifetime's worth of
> tight spots in the past—including Dick Morris, the 1996 campaign strategist who quit
> that post amid his own sex scandal (*Los Angeles Times*, January 27, 1998).

> When Gennifer Flowers sent the 1992 Clinton campaign to the precipice with her ac-
> count of a long-running affair with the Arkansas governor, the candidate dispatched
> a loyal, pugnacious lawyer with a highly attuned political ear to rescue his drive in
> New Hampshire: Mickey Kantor. Now, with his presidency threatened by accusations
> of an affair with a young White House intern, Bill Clinton has reached to the same
> hardened strategist to bring order to his defense and, if possible, find a way out of the
> toughest political crisis of his crisis-filled career (*New York Times*, January 27).

Such regular exposure keeps operatives in the news, cast in the sympathetic role
of political savior. They are, in a sense, the superheroes of politics, who create and
salvage political careers by effectively manipulating information; they have earned
their fame appropriately in an information-thirsty political environment. Press
coverage is filled with the fruits of their labor, with references to campaign strategy and the tactics designed to advance it. By highlighting the advisers themselves,
the media simply acknowledge that running for and holding office has become a
commercial enterprise, and campaign consultants are journalists' creations.

This is also the case when the media showcase campaign ads—a venue where
we are told that politics is a commercial endeavor in every sense of the word. Like
the hired guns who produce the commercials, paid campaign ads are hardly new
to the political arena. In Chapter 2 we saw how Dwight D. Eisenhower employed
advertising consultants for his successful 1952 presidential run and how television
ads have been used and refined ever since. However, in 1952 and for the next
twenty years, there was virtually no discussion of campaign ads in the press. This
began to change in the 1970s with the advent of television politics spawned by
campaign reform. Since 1972, there has been a sustained increase in the amount of
coverage devoted to political advertisements in such media as the *New York Times*,
the *Washington Post*, and CBS news programs.

The makeup of this coverage is interesting. An analysis by political scientist
Darrell M. West of the content of CBS news coverage of campaign ads between
1972 and 1992 suggests that political ads are most likely to address a candidate's

performance or policy views, whereas television coverage of political ads is predominantly about the campaign. During the twenty-year period, two-thirds of the CBS news stories about campaign ads were about the political horserace. And consistent with the media's militaristic approach to campaigns two-thirds of the ads appearing on CBS news programs were negative in tone (West, 1993).

Perhaps the best example of how advertising has become news is provided by Ross Perot's fall 1992 presidential campaign. Following his reentry into the presidential fray after dropping out the previous summer, the Texas billionaire did little but advertise on television. Ironically devoid of handlers owing to the candidate's tight control of his operation, the Perot campaign was almost entirely a series of television **infomercials,** generally thirty-minute ads running on network television in prime time. Backed by his massive fortune, Perot, in conjunction with the Texas advertising firm Temerlin McClain, purchased massive amounts of television time to use as a forum for getting out his message (*Washington Post,* October 2). Although Perot staged a few rallies as election day drew near, he never produced the daily whirlwind of activity typical of presidential candidates—and upon which reporters depend for news.

Consequently, in order to cover Perot, the media were forced to cover his version of presidential politics. As the *Dallas Morning News* put it, "Welcome to the Ross Perot campaign. Live! From a TV studio near you!" (October 8). In truth, it wasn't a great stretch for reporters to devote attention to a candidate who honored the medium of television in a way none before him had. If Perot, in the words of his coordinator Orson Swindle, "won't be going out kissing babies" (*Boston Globe,* October 6), reporters could readily find horserace excitement in the first truly commercial presidential campaign.

Perot himself framed his reentry into national politics in terms of his wish to buy television time, and he did so on national television. In response to a question about the economy asked by Jamie Gangel on the "Today" show, Perot sailed into his media-based reasoning for running: "If the television networks will sell me time, I'm going to be talking about this economy big time. . . . Interestingly enough I'm trapped; they won't sell it to me unless I declare as a candidate. So I may be the first guy in history that had to declare as a candidate so he could first buy TV time" (September 18).

Of course, the media responded to this because Perot was speaking their language. "A novel notion: the networks made me do it," chuckled *Newsweek* magazine over Perot's logic (September 28). But the candidate would have the next laugh. A host of coverage followed his reentry to the race, lending legitimacy to Perot's infomercial effort and credibility to the notion of presidential campaigns as sponsored, big-money affairs.

The first thirty-minute Perot program, a discussion of economic problems, aired October 6, 1992, on CBS at a cost of $380,000.[11] Press reaction was immediate and predictably emphasized the unconventional use of the medium rather than the substance of the infomercial. The *Washington Post* noted that the infomercial's "simple editing and lack of visuals . . . broke all the conventional rules for holding viewers' attention" (October 7). It "defied all political wisdom," observed the *Los Angeles Times* (October 7). "Like the old Superman serials," clucked CNN (October 6), in an outdated reference to a series that, like the Perot ads, would build on past episodes.

As the campaign progressed, the media came to regard the Perot television campaign as a factor in the larger horserace. Accordingly, coverage of his ads took on a competitive tone. NBC news observed that "Perot has shown he can attract viewers but according to the polls not voters" (October 17). The *New York Times* suggested that Perot was unleashing a new set of ads in order to build on his growing political "momentum" (October 22). In the campaign's final days, Lisa Myers went so far as to assess for her NBC audience the differences between the person viewers saw on the commercials—the "purchased" Perot—and the one who at that point had called his credibility into question with a series of far-fetched allegations about his opponents. Myers said :

> Admen say the jarring difference between the Perot many saw on the news this week and the man in his ads will undercut the ads' effectiveness. [Sound bite of advertising consultant saying "The voters will reject a candidate if there's conflict in the messages that they're getting because it means that there's something wrong."] The conflict between fact and fiction goes to the heart of the Perot campaign (October 28).

The mention of "admen" in Myers's story is instructive. Not only had commercial advertising made possible an entire presidential campaign, and not only had the media legitimated the commercials by incorporating them in their regular coverage, but the people who produce ads for a living had been elevated to the status of official source. Of course, it all makes sense: Who better than professionals to assess the impact of their product? Had coverage been about policy debate, NBC likely would have presented us with an economist. In the 1990s, advertising agents can be expected to stand on the same platform in an honest admission of how political coverage tells us of the buying and selling of American politics.

## The Public: Prisoners of War?

At the height of the Monica Lewinsky frenzy, Ted Koppel made this observation in a discussion with his colleague Cokie Roberts: "Sometimes we [in the press] get too concerned with what we think within the [Washington, D.C.,] Beltway. We don't pay enough attention to what people are saying out beyond Washington" (ABC, "Nightline," January 27, 1998). He has a point. Washington politics is often about manipulation. But when manipulation dominates the political news frame, the audience is treated to a dubious picture of democracy. Seen through this frame, the only way politicians advance or survive is by means of distortion and deceit, which are documented in great detail. We are presented with little material that would temper messages about political scratching and clawing because the frame of reference for campaign coverage is fixed on the candidate-media game.

Not surprisingly, negative coverage has increased as the campaign frame has shifted from the candidates to the media, from electoral competition to duplicity in the name of political gain. The political scientist Thomas Patterson has tracked the number of favorable, or "good news," items about major-party candidates written by reporters for *Time* and *Newsweek* between 1960 and 1992 in relation to "bad news." His findings are illustrated in Figure 3.4. In every election before 1980, good news outdistanced the bad. But in three of the next four elections, just the opposite occurred. Whereas three of four references to Kennedy and Nixon in 1960 were positive, the comparable figure was 40 percent for Clinton and Bush in 1992. This decline captures the negative nature of campaign reporting framed in terms of media politics.

The increased negativity also closely parallels a widely held public perspective on politics. According to political scientist Doris Graber, Americans commonly process news coverage by organizing it around existing cognitive structures, each of which is called a **schema** (in the plural, schemata). Graber finds commonly held schemata to include a "generally negative view of government and politicians" and a "strong belief that on balance the American system is sound" (Graber, 1988: p. 257). Given how the media portray politics, neither of these cognitive structures is surprising. Although reporters rarely question the validity of American democracy or the process by which it operates (by, for instance, raising doubts about the American system), they constantly call into question the actions and motivation of its political participants.

If news coverage were just a mirror of preexisting attitudes about politics, then it could be argued that we are simply getting what we want: a campaign picture that dovetails cleanly with widely held negative views of political actors. But there is strong evidence that patterns of learning from news coverage closely parallel political reporters' frame of reference, and this suggests at the very least that negative reporting perpetuates negative attitudes. Studies demonstrate that citizens achieve limited knowledge of candidates and their issue positions from consuming election coverage and are likely to structure what they learn around the horserace politics of the campaign. Sampling from a limited political menu, peo-

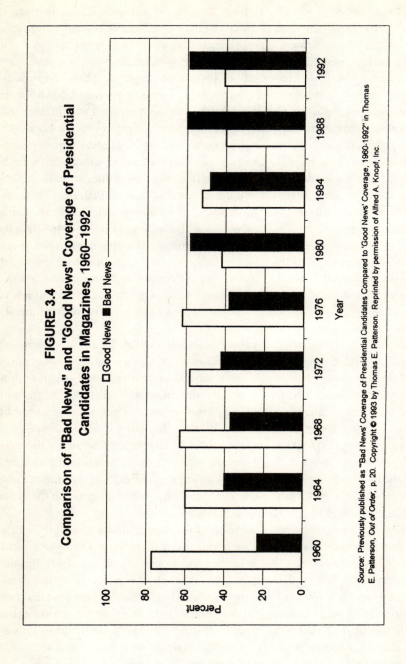

**FIGURE 3.4**

**Comparison of "Bad News" and "Good News" Coverage of Presidential Candidates in Magazines, 1960–1992**

☐ Good News  ■ Bad News

Year

Percent

*Source:* Previously published as "'Bad News' Coverage of Presidential Candidates Compared to 'Good News' Coverage, 1960-1992" in Thomas E. Patterson, *Out of Order*, p. 20. Copyright © 1993 by Thomas E. Patterson. Reprinted by permission of Alfred A. Knopf, Inc.

ple remember the fare that exists in abundance and quite naturally reflect on the meal in terms of the food that was served rather than the dishes that were not (Popkin, 1991; Joslyn, 1984; Keeter and Zukin 1983; Patterson, 1980).

Besides, there is evidence of some public appetite for greater variety. When left to their own devices, citizens will ask candidates about where they stand on the issues. Despite widespread disaffection with politicians, they will take candidates seriously enough to listen to their answers. And they tend not to ask the sort of horserace, strategy, or personality questions that obsess political reporters.

Voters like the individual interviewed by NBC in New Hampshire were permitted during the general election campaign to ask questions of George Bush, Bill Clinton, and Ross Perot in an unprecedented Phil Donahue–style debate held October 15, 1992. After getting the candidates to agree not to snipe at one another, audience members asked questions about the economy, homelessness, unemployment, abortion, and other issue-oriented matters not typically a political reporter's primary concern.

Postdebate coverage acknowledged the substantive questioning but, in quintessential horserace fashion, framed the debate in terms of winners and losers. Voter-questioners were interested in the economy; postdebate analysis emphasized the unique format that had made the debate, in the words of USA Today, "live but not lively." Television pundits babbled about how well Bill Clinton understood their medium:

> NBC: The format was terrific for [Clinton].
> ABC: Clinton commanded the atmospherics . . . [and] was more aware of what this television format was than either of his opponents.
> CBS: This was Bill Clinton being his most presidential.
> CNN: Clinton clearly was a master of the format.

Once the event was over, the details of what was said were relegated to history, appearing only collectively in subsequent media references to how, unlike journalists, citizen-questioners liked to talk about something vaguely called "the issues." This distinction is validated by the content of horserace coverage, which shows how political reporters value the war more than the words. The New York Times said of the October debate: "Historic it was. Also responsible, civic-minded, worthwhile and informative. Also dull as C-SPAN at midnight." More to the point was the San Francisco Examiner headline that declared the event to have been the "electronic town meeting from hell."

That citizens ask politicians issue-based questions indicates the existence of some level of public interest in the substance of elections and reflects a discrepancy with the values of political reporters. The public may process political information through schemata that follow the reporter's cynical frame and still have the capacity or desire for some degree of substantive instruction. Not surprisingly, studies indicate that more political learning takes place from debate forums and from political ads—two readily available sources of information—than from election news coverage (Just et al., 1990; Joslyn, 1984; Patterson and McClure, 1976). Once reporters get hold of debates and advertisements and digest them for the audience, the horserace stories that predictably emerge have far less useful information content. In these instances, news reports ostensibly offered to inform the larger audience prove far less meaningful than the events they purportedly attempt to explain.

Of course, savoring the contest is not mutually exclusive to being interested in issues and wishing to learn more about what the candidates propose to do in office. People may want both; certainly, if editors and producers need verification that there is an appetite for horserace news, it may be found in the size of the audience that regularly consumes it. Media economics are such that if horserace coverage made audiences run, it would readily be replaced with something different. Although news producers and editors are wont to misunderstand the makeup of the audience, believing erroneously that viewers share their socioeconomic characteristics and political interests, they have a point when they argue that a viewer revolt against political news has yet to materialize (Kerbel, 1998; Gans, 1979).

However, although large, that audience may be disengaged. Unlike the active processing that can accompany learning about substantive issues, watching news about the contest is in all likelihood a far more passive activity. In a study of the 1976 presidential race, individuals were asked to recall and react to an election story they had heard the previous day. People most frequently remembered horserace news but generally did not react to it. News about policy and issues, albeit less readily available and therefore less frequently recalled, was nonetheless far more likely to generate citizen response (Patterson, 1980). We are lulled by the horserace; it is political coverage for the couch potato.

It should not be surprising, therefore, that horserace coverage largely omits the public at large, leaving us to our own devices as passive viewers of a story ostensibly about somebody else. Despite the tendency to personalize politics and elections, political coverage contains remarkably few references to the persons who benefit or suffer from political decisions: those in the public who will decide the outcome of elections and who will live with their choices. In television's account of the 1992 presidential campaign, voters rarely appeared as the subject of news stories. In coverage of the Lewinsky scandal, the public was mentioned primarily in terms of its outrage at the poor quality of news reporting. Both are passive representations of citizenship, projecting an image of viewers that was true to the passive manner in which political coverage is received (Kerbel, 1998).

## Conclusion

In the war that is media coverage of politics, viewers sit on the sidelines receiving battlefield pictures and commentary. Arguably, if politics were a war, this is precisely where the viewer would wish to be and exactly how the public would be portrayed. Generals and their soldiers would do the public's bidding, planning strategy and implementing tactics, retreating when necessary, reevaluating in the face of setbacks. The outcome would affect the common good, and some people might mobilize to write letters to public officials or demonstrate in favor of or against the action. However, the event would gravitate toward conclusion without direct involvement from the public at large.

But we are talking about politics, not a war. Citizens do have a meaningful direct role in the outcome. The stakes are high, but consequences are not lethal. Candidate behavior is important, but cast in a somewhat less ultimate perspective, candidates could make mistakes and display human frailties without being subjected to the sort of treatment that ultimately casts a pall over the entire political process. Those who wish to cast their ballots on the basis of a candidate's improprieties would still be informed enough to do so. It doesn't take much creativity to see where those shortcomings lie. It takes far more imagination for the public to find virtue in a process that the media relentlessly portray in negative terms.

# 4

.........................................................................

# Presidential Governance and Other Fantasies

[Covering government] has become a kind of massive
game of "gotcha.". . . We look for every little tiny flaw
and when we can't find it, then what we do is examine
what we haven't been able to find and say, "But what if?"

—Tom Brokaw, NBC News,
interviewed on CNBC, May 9, 1993

Editors don't want to run [misconduct stories] without
proof, yet once they are injected into the public
consciousness, and the legal process, the editors can't
pretend they're not out there. It is a dilemma not
satisfactorily solved either by ignoring the stories or
jumping on the bandwagon.

—Jack Germond and Jules Witcover,
*Baltimore Sun,* May 10, 1993

To HEAR REPORTERS TELL IT, they are caught in a bind. Nobody wants to engage in irresponsible or irrelevant coverage, but everybody is part of a system that permits trivia and sideshow to inform the main political event. So long as what Tom Brokaw calls "gotcha" stories are permissible in mainstream media, competitive pressures will guarantee that skeptical stories about political officials will be, in the words of Germond and Witcover, "out there"—a part of public consciousness. Neither overlooking these stories nor joining the frenzy may be an acceptable alternative for thoughtful journalists, but given a choice between the two, reporters definitely won't ignore the stories. That would entail being left out of the hunt. Reporters have shown a proclivity instead to engage in coverage they feel questionable, then publicly confess their sins after the fact through newspaper columns or television talk shows.

The soul-searching, of course, changes neither the system nor the makeup of political news. We should not expect it to. The content of coverage is determined by far more than simply how reporters act. It is part of the much larger process we explored in Chapters 2 and 3, facilitated in no small measure by history, technology, and institutional reform.

Brokaw, Germond, and Witcover could have been talking about coverage of political contests. In fact, each was ruminating over media attention given to sexual harassment charges leveled against President Clinton by Paula Jones, and how coverage of the charges had, momentarily at least, diverted media attention from legislative efforts to reform health care. In other words, their concern was coverage of governance and the actions of political figures in official roles. That their words could easily apply to campaign news is important because it illustrates how the competitive, combative perspective of political reporting has infiltrated coverage of how the nation is governed.

This policy-as-politics frame supplies us with good reason to feel alienated from government and skeptical about the people charged with writing and executing the law. Repeatedly, the media approach governance as if it were electoral politics, applying the same horserace-oriented, character-based, scandal-laden coverage standards to news about policy debate and development. We are cued to look for winners and losers, to see the legislative process—in truth a cumbersome, lethargic, complex system driven by the deeds of hundreds if not thousands of individuals—as a backdrop to an overly simplified tug-of-war between the president and Congress.

The purpose behind policymaking, we are told, is for the president to enhance his stature and prestige by proving his effectiveness through winning legislative victories. Scandals may intervene and sidetrack the effort; presidential strategy (much like candidate strategy) may vary in effectiveness as the chief executive pushes toward his goal. The horserace is monitored through head counts in Congress: the gain of a crucial vote here, the surprising loss of a onetime supporter there—all calculated for the education of the home audience. The behavior of every party to the process, especially the president and members of Congress, is readily reduced to petty, personal, political terms.

The costs and benefits of the proposals under consideration are frequently framed in the same political manner. Substantive discussion of major issues like health care reform tends to focus on which groups stand to benefit from or be hurt by prospective changes, their support or opposition approached in terms of how likely it is to facilitate or hinder the president's objectives. Although policy decisions produce winners and losers, the value of debate and discussion lies in scrutinizing the major arguments on different sides of an issue so as to build consensus around a particular course of action if agreement can, in fact, be reached. This perspective is lost to the viewer when position-taking is defined in terms of how it changes the odds of a particular outcome, and when interest groups are pejoratively portrayed in terms of their lobbying efforts to block a provision or protect a stake.

Compounding the disparagement of governance is the disparity between the policy process portrayed by the media and the constitutional system designed centuries ago. Under that system, power is institutionalized and decentralized among the branches to impede progress. But media coverage of governance suggests that power is personalized and absolute, that it resides in a form of presidential government promising fast results and immediate progress. This image is at odds with institutional design, at odds with reality.

The system was fashioned to be what political scientist Austin Ranney calls "a government of conflicting parts," one designed to frustrate action rather than to risk imposing on the whole the wishes of a few:

> The men of 1787 built many well-conceived and effective devices into the formal constitutional system to achieve their goals. They divided the national government's power among its three branches and they prohibited any person from serving in more than one branch at a time. They provided that the persons occupying the leading offices in each branch would serve for terms of different lengths, be selected by different constituencies, and be chosen at sufficiently different intervals that there would never be a

British-style "general election" in which all the officeholders could be swept out of office on a wave of strong though temporary popular passion. And they crowned the system with an elaborate set of checks and balances to ensure that each branch could delay or prevent action by the other branches (Ranney, 1983: p. 137).

But an observer would never gather any of this from media coverage of the policy process. Despite the reality of divided government, presidential leadership is assumed to be the standard. Despite the manner in which power is decentralized across institutions to give many actors a say over outcomes, personalities are emphasized over processes. The agenda is always the president's, and his strength is measured by his ability to get his way with Congress. Fast action is the mark of presidential success; delay or defeat is a sign of weakness.

That the system is not designed to work this way is irrelevant. Constitutional design meshes poorly with the realities of contemporary media, which favor people over procedure, presidents over Congresses, and results over deliberation. Gridlock between the executive and legislative branches is "bad," even though it is one of the system's greatest safeguards against foolish or dangerous action, and even though it is a far more commonplace outcome than fast action.

When reality frequently fails to meet reporter expectations, coverage acquires the language of disappointment and defeat. This slant makes it hard to ferret through reports of setback and failure without asking reasonable questions about exactly what is going on in Washington. Even if the citizen's intent is to be informed about the details of a policy being debated and discussed, the way governance is framed in the press ensures this information will be conveyed along with doubtful messages about the state of the system. It is possible, even rational, for the citizen to be educated—and put off.

Because media coverage is part of a larger system involving other players, the governance-as-horserace frame is reinforced from several directions. Presidents play to the media in an effort to win favorable coverage, much as presidential candidates attempt to control the terms of election news. Public perceptions of presidential effectiveness can have a powerful impact on others in the Washington community and boost a president's legislative prospects. Getting the best of media coverage can enhance legislators' stature[1] and thus render presidential media strategy ever more critical to the governing process. Members of Congress in recent years have also found television's bright lights hard to resist, and as the institution has become awash in media attention, many of its members have taken to the airwaves to carve out their point of view for the national audience (Ornstein, 1983).

This self-promotion serves to make governance more problematic because it reinforces the unrealistic impression of the system portrayed in the media. Consequently, reporters are given even more reason to relate discouraging news about the process. A senator's sound bite on the evening news expressing doubt about his support of a key provision of a policy initiative is readily framed by reporters as "a grave setback" to the administration's efforts. A presidential public relations event designed to rally public support to a particular cause is analyzed in the news as a cynical and questionable ploy. By casting doubt on the motives of the key players and on the consequences of their actions, the media do more than give the appearance of government stalemate and ineffectiveness. They actually make it harder to govern.

In the pages ahead, we will examine the details of the governance-as-horserace frame in terms of how three groups with an investment in the system are afforded coverage: the president, Congress, and interest groups. We will look first at how the policy process is portrayed from a presidential perspective, with themes borrowed from political campaigns. By revisiting the NAFTA initiative outlined in Chapter 1 and by considering coverage of the 1994 national health care debate, we will see how the media accentuate familiar horserace themes that favor strategy and sideshow over issue discussion. Similarly, we will examine the reflexive nature of policy coverage that, like election coverage, features the press as an important actor in its own story. Then we will use examples from health care stories to illustrate how Congress and interest groups are covered. The former, in contrast to its central position in the legislative process, is typically seen as secondary or, worse, as an impediment to the president's objectives. The latter are framed in terms of how their lobbying efforts influence the political battle rather than in relation to arguably more important issues, such as how their efforts influence resource allocation. We will conclude by considering the public's stake in governance and how media coverage might make it difficult for us to evaluate government's effectiveness.

## The President: Impotence Despite Omnipotence

Turn on the television and watch the president chat with Larry King, live from the White House. Or watch the chief executive hold a televised "town meeting" to address his health care reform initiative. Perhaps he's on a morning "infotainment" program like "Good Morning America" or "Today." Most certainly he can be found somewhere on the evening news.

Television makes it seem as if the president is everywhere because television and the modern presidency share a symbiotic relationship. The single representative of the federal government is the most readily available symbol for a pictorial medium, which surpasses all other vehicles for delivering to the president an instantaneous mass audience. Simply put, television is able to cover the presidency more effectively and more extensively than it can cover any multiple-member institution because the presidency may be portrayed in terms of a single person appearing on camera amid the symbolic trappings of the office. Presidents craving a public platform eagerly play to this tendency, fueling the appearance that national government is presidential government—that all policy originates at the White House, moves through or stalls in Congress because of presidential competence or ineffectiveness, and becomes law in response to presidential initiative.[2]

The presidency and television have grown up together. As we saw in Chapter 2, the postwar world produced unparalleled international responsibilities for America and a new electronic network for connecting once-distant parts of a vast nation. America's new role as nuclear power and world leader focused attention on the commander in chief, naturally elevating the president to the forefront of international dialogue. Television obliged by affording the president unprecedented exposure. Power had already begun shifting from localities to the federal level with the advent of Franklin D. Roosevelt's New Deal social programs in the 1930s; the emergence of America on the world stage reinforced this trend and guaranteed that through television, Americans would come to think of the government in presidential terms.

By the early 1950s, astute politicians and operatives were already recognizing the ramifications of being able to reach a mass audience. The Kefauver crime hearings and the Murrow-McCarthy confrontation drove home the effects of bringing elected officials and policy matters into homes across the country. Shortly, policy discussion would be nationalized as a matter of course, and the president's words would come to symbolize for many the state of the nation (Stuckey, 1991).

In the 1960s and 1970s, the tendency toward presidential government was facilitated by the decline in the power of the party elites discussed in Chapter 3. The long primary campaigns that replaced elite candidate selection are personality-centered, televised events. Candidates ask the people for support, making whatever promises necessary to win the votes that could hand them the nomination of their party. Once in office, they are held by the public (and the media) to their promises, a natural extension of the "personal" relationship developed on television during the campaign.

Of course, the television presidency operates on television's terms. As the medium personalizes government, so does it accelerate it and politicize it. Skillful presidents have learned how to use the medium to communicate their version of events to the nation, but this advantage is balanced by the rapidity with which presidents in the television age are expected to accomplish objectives and by the self-serving political manner in which their actions are cast.

Television coverage places the burden of action on the president and compresses the amount of time available to produce results. Austin Ranney notes television's "insatiable appetite for news stories" (Ranney, 1983: p. 127), which is to say news defined as something unique. When events do not keep pace with this demand, television will build stories around proxies, such as monthly economic indicators or, in recent years, national opinion poll figures. This forces the president to make progress—or at least give the appearance of making progress. When network-sponsored opinion polls show the president's job approval to be declining or support for his major policy initiatives dwindling, the White House feels real pressure to do something to get the numbers back up. When approval is high, the pressure is equally great for the president to maintain it.

The problem for the president is that he operates in a system that affords him limited ability to meet these expectations single-handedly. The open, personalized, presidential view of the legislative process portrayed on television is at odds with the complex internal, bureaucratized, congressional mechanism that actually evaluates policy options and writes the law. Television may have opened the legislative process to millions of American homes, but it has not changed the institutional restrictions that make progress difficult and change slow (Barilleaux, 1988). It may have personalized governance by putting faces to the process, but many egos and interests reside within the congressional talking heads appearing on the screen. The president is still only one player, and contrary to what television suggests, he doesn't always hold the best cards.

Moreover, what it takes to win election in a television campaign confounds the job of governing. Candidates are forced to inflate their promises beyond what was once necessary in order to win primary votes in all regions of the country. Candidates, in essence, must make numerous individual pacts with many interests in order to pull together enough support to win nomination. In the past, the elite-based system permitted candidates to forge coalitions with groups loyal to the party. These could be called upon by the new president to help with the task of governance. As television replaced parties as the primary link to the voters, and as media handlers replaced party leaders as key electoral intermediaries, personal popularity supplanted governing coalitions as the president's greatest postelection resource (Lowi, 1985; Rubin, 1981).

This personal aura is a slender and unpredictable asset in the face of elevated performance standards. Ironically, some of the same forces that make the president more dependent on popularity also make public support of the president more unstable than in the past. As the presidency has moved to the forefront of the political system, and as media-magnified presidential rhetoric has increased, presidents have been less convincing under greater and more aggressive press scrutiny. Political scientist Richard Rubin describes what he calls the "unmooring" of once-stable presidential popularity, a shift facilitated by a newfound misplaced emphasis on presidential image. Despite the president's unprecedented ability to command a media platform, image is a highly volatile quality rapidly undermined by negative coverage. Rubin describes the Carter presidency as "an increasingly rapid roller coaster of ups and downs of public confidence in his leadership" (Rubin, 1981: p. 220). Little more than a decade later, George Bush realized unprecedented public approval in the wake of the Persian Gulf War—the year before he was voted out of office. Two decades later, the Clinton administration traveled a road replete with sharp peaks and valleys in popular support.

In this volatile environment, it is easy for people to lose faith in presidents. Many readers, for instance, would be convinced with little persuasion that presidents blithely make pledges just to get elected, promises they have no intention to keep. Sometimes this is true; there is evidence, for instance, that President Clinton had little regard for the middle-class tax cut he promised as a candidate yet saw it as a necessary way to get middle-class votes (Woodward, 1994). But it defies reason that candidates would say *anything* to get elected; they know they will be scrutinized once in power. Evidence suggests that candidates have a strong desire to fulfill campaign promises and that the positions offered in party platforms are good indicators of what candidates have tried to do in office (Patterson, 1993; Pomper, 1973).

The key word here is "tried." Because the electoral system requires elevated rhetoric, presidents commit to do what the mediated version of governance leads the public to believe they can do—and that is far more than they can realistically achieve. Political scientist Theodore Lowi makes the point: "Presidents spend the first half of their terms trying sincerely to succeed according to their oath and their promises. They devote the second half of their terms trying to create the appearance of success" (Lowi, 1985: p. 11). This, of course, requires even more rhetoric. If they are unconvincing, or if people tire of their words, they lose public support and potentially their jobs. But we replace them with other candidates offering even more and better outcomes because we tend to believe the person, not the system, is malfunctioning. That is the message we get from the media.

Complicating matters further is the tendency for television to regard governance as politics and to cover the development of legislation as if it were a presidential campaign. Performance-based standards emphasize the process by which policy is shaped; with the president in the lead, he is evaluated for his capacity to govern in terms of the speed with which the legislative process moves toward approving what is invariably regarded as "his" program. This emphasis, too, is at odds with the reality of a process designed to retard initiative and is of questionable benefit to the viewing audience.

Nonetheless, television's model has become the journalistic norm. Other media in recent years have fallen in line behind television's political standard, emphasizing the presidential role in governance and assessing presidential performance by the same political benchmarks. Media portray the president as legislator in chief and analyze the legislative process in the shorthand of who is up and who is down. Quite often, given the complex nature of that process, it is the president who is down.

All the components of political news we addressed in Chapter 3 reappear in coverage of governance. As they do with campaigns, the media frame governance as a sequence of policy initiatives put forth by the president in which presidential success (more so than public policy) is at stake. Legislation substitutes for electoral victory; legislative votes double for electoral votes. To achieve a "win" (and thereby enhance his popularity and status as an ever-desirable "strong" president), the president is portrayed much like a candidate posturing, employing strategies derivative of campaigns to gain advantage over opponents of the measure in question, attempting not to be sidetracked by character issues that could deflect media attention from the matter at hand and undermine momentum for the bill. Horserace references outpace substantive issue discussion. Even the warroom handlers are back, trying to manage yet another victory.

Examples of this frame may be found in the Clinton administration's 1993 initiative to win congressional approval of NAFTA and in the 1994 debate over health care reform. Both policy undertakings were covered as political events featuring the president. Even though much of the action (and all of the voting) occurred in Congress, the president was portrayed as the one with the most political chips at stake, and enhancing his political position was characterized as a potential outcome of great consequence.

The audience was cued to the highs and lows of presidential fortune as each initiative wound its way through the turbulent legislative process. Wolf Blitzer dutifully reported to the CNN audience that November 9, 1993, "was a very good day for NAFTA," according to his White House sources, "and they expect another good day [today]." One week later, presidential counselor David Gergen appeared on both the "Today" show and CBS "This Morning" to offer the latest White House line on the NAFTA horserace: "For the first time, the pro-NAFTA forces have caught up with the anti-NAFTA forces. And the momentum is clearly and decisively on the side of the pro-NAFTA forces" (CBS, "This Morning," November 16). Those same programs reinforced Gergen's talk of campaignlike "momentum" with reporter accounts of Gergen's comment. On CBS, Bill Plante noted, in the language of television, "The White House was very busy yesterday spinning the notion that there has been a shift in momentum in the president's favor." His

NBC counterpart Jim Miklaszewski acknowledged, "The opponents are slightly ahead, but the momentum is clearly on the president's side" (November 16).

Low points were dutifully reported as well. On November 4, in the wake of the 1993 election that replaced Democrats with Republicans in a high-profile mayoral race in New York City and a gubernatorial race in New Jersey, pundits were quick to predict (incorrectly, it turned out) negative fallout for the president's NAFTA efforts. Analyst Charles Cook was quoted in the *Dallas Morning News* as saying, "To the extent that willingness to do something to help the president was low, it just got lower. I don't know how you could look at yesterday's results and feel better about voting for [NAFTA]." Democratic strategist Mark Siegel offered this analysis, reported in *New York Newsday:* "If I represent a blue-collar constituency and the president says to me, 'You have to do what's right for the country even though it may have short-term negative impact politically,' I can say, 'Yeah, tell that to [defeated New Jersey Governor] Jim Florio.'" Republican pollster Vince Breglio concurred, telling the *Wall Street Journal,* "I think NAFTA is dead, and Tuesday's results were the final nail in the coffin."

As these predictions proved off the mark in the coming weeks and legislative approval of the trade pact remained possible, analysts and reporters began to comment on the competitive nature of the "race" and on the prospects for presidential "victory" in Congress. Washington insiders, on such forums as CNN's "Capital Gang" and "The McLaughlin Group," filled airtime by handicapping the race as the final vote approached. The closing question posed to the McLaughlin panel on November 13 typifies the discussion. Asked, simply, "Will NAFTA pass?" the assembled commentators responded as if they were betting on the Super Bowl. Fred Barnes: "NAFTA by uno." Eleanor Clift: "NAFTA by trois." Jack Germond: "219–215 for NAFTA." Morton Kondracke: "It gets 218 votes and no more." John McLaughlin: "219–215 for NAFTA."

Handicapping was not limited to programs designed for political junkies. This colorful insider prediction of the NAFTA vote scenario could be heard on CNN's "Late Edition":

> This [vote] is going to come down to two or three minutes on the clock [in the House of Representatives], probably around ten at night. And you'll see 213 [votes] up there. And [House Speaker] Tom Foley and [Republican Whip] Newt Gingrich . . . are going to have to get 218. They're going to go, "Now where are they?" If they don't keep those guys on the floor, they won't be able to find them. So the Republicans have corralled twenty guys, Newt Gingrich's young guys, and they'll say, "You stay put. We're going to see if the Democrats hit the 100 mark. If they hit the 100 mark, I'll release you twenty guys [to vote for NAFTA]. Otherwise, we're not playing ball." Because the Republicans are not going to be the horse in the horse-and-rabbit stew. They want this thing to be relatively equal (November 14).

Predictions that didn't emphasize the final numbers nonetheless anticipated the president's political position should the bill face defeat. The predictions were dire and reflected the deep political meaning ascribed to policy outcomes. David Broder wrote in the *Washington Post* that a loss on NAFTA "would reduce [President Clinton's] international standing to a point unparalleled since Richard Nixon was careening toward resignation" (November 14). *Business Week* imagined "pundits . . . declaring the Clinton presidency a Carteresque flop" (November 22). Added columnist Fred Barnes, "If NAFTA goes down President Clinton will be in, metaphorically speaking, the same condition John Bobbitt was in after the attack" (CNN, "The McLaughlin Group," November 13). As with coverage of presidential campaigns, the worst-case scenario is depicted as far more than simple defeat.

Comments about the inner workings of the White House complemented these horserace predictions, similarly emphasizing political conditions and concerns, at times highlighting the difficulties of forging an effective legislative drive. For instance, given the dynamics of domestic policy development, one might expect that Clinton's ambitious legislative agenda would naturally be difficult to advance. Divisions between the White House and Congress and even within the president's own staff could be predicted on such things as NAFTA and health care reform. But the following *Wall Street Journal* piece views such differences in the context of presidential leadership, raising doubts about Clinton's abilities while offering readers a perspective on the nastier aspects of working in the White House.

> The strain of tackling both the health and trade issues at the same time is sparking dissension and back-biting between the officials charged with delivering on each—and those tensions have invaded the highest echelons of the administration. . . . By not setting a clear priority, the president has renewed complaints that he is unable or unwilling to provide presidential leadership, even over his own administration and Democratic party. . . . The sniping has become so bad . . . [that senior White House aides] met separately with advocates of each issue in an effort to end the bickering (September 3).

Whether presidential leadership could put an end to backbiting is debatable. Internal sniping was a staple of life in the executive branch under presidents whose control of internal matters was undisputed. George Reedy, who worked in the Johnson administration, said the White House assistant's constant quest for advantage over his peers "resembles nothing else known in the world except possibly the Japanese game of *go,* a contest in which there are very few fixed rules and the playing consists of laying down alternating counters in patterns that permit flexibility but seek to deny that flexibility to the opponent" (Reedy, 1987: p. 78). This may be a more useful frame of reference for the NAFTA and health care disputes. A close reading of the *Journal* piece reveals that policy differences mask personality conflicts, with NAFTA supporters "especially frustrated with health care czar Ira Magaziner, whom they accuse of being secretive and excessively turf conscious." It is hardly realistic to believe this conflict either would not continue or would be replaced with another one had the president decided to emphasize one initiative over the other. To the contrary, loss of turf on either side would be a catalyst for greater struggle.

In Lyndon Johnson's day, such inside struggles were not prominently covered despite being evident to the press. Then, as now, it was "business as usual" in a setting where the power stakes are enormous. But as the story of policymaking has essentially become a story about power, White House office politics inevitably receives media attention. Portraying power struggles among aides in terms of ineffective presidential leadership may be debatable, but it is hardly surprising.

News about in-house bickering is consistent with the thematic component of policy coverage emphasizing how the president is trying to achieve his objectives. As with election reporting, the media devote considerable attention to strategic maneuvering, interpreting for the audience the methodology of successful governance. Cast against the uphill struggle that (understandably) characterizes much policy formulation, stories about executive salesmanship are offered in great numbers as a framework for interpreting presidential behavior.

Once reporters like CBS news correspondent Rita Braver begin asserting that "the health care struggle is getting pretty ugly and very political" (December 3, 1993), strategic coverage becomes an inevitable method for telling the audience what the president was going to do to work the politics to his advantage. In general terms, we learn when the administration "revved up the offensive" (CBS, "Evening News," September 16, 1993) or put its "campaign to sell health care reform . . . in full swing" (CNN, September 16). Specifically, we are told such subtle things as why the president—in a televised appearance on "CBS This Morning"— had begun referring to health care alliances as "cooperatives": In the search for "a new way to sell its ideas," the administration was "reaching back to a description that White House strategists initially rejected because they feared it sounded too bureaucratic and socialistic" (*New York Times*, March 4, 1994). Or we are educated to the purpose behind a White House attack on the insurance industry: "According to senior officials, the White House wanted a scapegoat. It also wanted to deflect attention from the fact that 40 percent of Americans will pay more under the Clinton plan" (NBC, "Nightly News," November 11, 1993).

Presidents, aware of the ability to use the media to mobilize public support, contribute their share to strategic coverage by staging events in order to build momentum for their cause. The strategy of **going public**—of building popular support so as to pressure senators and representatives—lends itself naturally to televised marketing. In recent years, new media options have provided presidents with an unprecedented variety of possibilities for reaching out to constituents, including televised forums through which they can circumvent the press entirely and appeal directly to the public. Given the campaign atmosphere surrounding the development and execution of these events, a political frame of reference is inevitable—and appropriate. The tactics are, in effect, campaign activities transplanted to government, an analogy that lends credence to the mediated view of governance as politics (Kernell, 1986; Barilleaux 1988).

In the Clinton administration, the options have even been implemented by campaign operatives. Days into his administration, facing a testy Congress tepid to his ambitious policy agenda, President Clinton brought into governance the political advisers who had successfully waged his 1992 electoral effort. This fact did not escape the self-referential media, which predictably reported in February 1993 that handlers James Carville and Paul Begala, the media wizards of 1992, were "now regularly involved in the [administration's policy] effort" (*Baltimore Sun*, February 7, 1993), leading figures in a presidential version of the campaign war room. The Executive Office Building quarters housing the new war room may have been more upscale than the campaign edition, and the purpose of the presidential version (to advance Clinton's domestic policy agenda) dramatically different from the previous year's campaign effort. But the tactics were as similar as the people who employed them. Aside from the newfound trappings of power, the resurrection of the war room made it hard to tell where the Clinton campaign ended and the Clinton administration began.

In fact, the campaign personnel were brought in by the Clinton administration specifically to apply campaign tactics to governing. The televised "**town meeting**," like the MTV forum discussed in Chapter 1, is one method they employed. A natural step beyond the reporterless, often favorable setting offered by televised talk shows, town meetings permit Clinton enormous control over events by making him the talk show host. Modeled after the New England town meeting where citizens meet in a hall to discuss directly matters of immediate concern, the mass version relies on satellite technology to beam a studio discussion between the president and a small number of participants to a national or regional audience. Viewers are invited to phone the president, who answers a small number of calls during the program.

Events like these play out on television and receive coverage in the press, compounding the importance of the media to governing. Coverage typically cues the audience to think of the strategic purpose of the event; television networks in particular like to emphasize the tactical use of their medium. This was evident in coverage of a barrage of television "conversations" about health care with the

President Clinton acts as "Donahue-in-chief" as he assumes the role of talk show host during a nationally televised town meeting on health care. Photo courtesy Reuters/ Bettmann.

president and Hillary Rodham Clinton held in September 1993. ABC explained the purpose behind the events: "The idea was to dramatize the problems for which Mr. Clinton will unveil his proposed solution next week" (September 16). NBC's Tom Brokaw, in a comment that implicitly equates media democracy with direct involvement, noted wryly, "You get the impression that sooner or later, [the Clintons] will come to your home to personally explain their plans to change health care in America" (September 16). Added Andrea Mitchell, in an apt reference to the melding of political executive and master of ceremonies, the televised format offers "Clinton as Donahue."

Other coverage specifically told citizens they were pawns in a televised sales campaign designed by the president to pressure Congress. The *New York Times* noted that Clinton advisers "are convinced that the secret to success for his health care program lies in taking his appeals beyond [Washington]. But [Clinton] has to woo members of Congress as well, so he has embarked on a double-barreled strategy" (April 8, 1994). Likewise, NBC coverage explained that "the White House is convinced [town meetings] are still the best way for the president to cut through the organized opposition back in Washington" (April 8).

Regardless of expert opinion, the sales job continued, at times assuming other equally familiar campaign forms. The televised debate is one prominent variation on the image and information control effort of the town meeting, also borrowed from the campaign and covered by the press in strategic horserace terms. It was employed by the Clinton administration in the days prior to the congressional vote on NAFTA as a modern-day vehicle for going public. The strategy called for Vice President Gore to be the administration's representative and Clinton's surrogate in a televised confrontation with Ross Perot, the most vocal NAFTA opponent. The confrontation would take place on CNN's "Larry King Live," with the host as moderator and open telephone lines for viewers to call in with questions.

When Connie Chung of CBS asked President Clinton about the wisdom of a strategy that pitted the vice president against a political loose cannon, the president responded, "Look, everything's a risk. We're living in a time of high change and great anxiety and profound cynicism, and I don't think running from the people is the best way to [govern]" (November 9, 1993). But the strategy entailed at worst a controlled risk (Clinton's acknowledgment of a possible Gore debacle bespoke an administration effort to lower expectations of the outcome, thereby minimizing the damage if Gore performed poorly). And the president was somewhat disingenuous to assert that a debate seen only on cable television was the antidote to "running from the people." Larry King was not regarded as a tough questioner, the debate would not air on network television, and a thicket of White House spin doctors was prepared to go to work on the journalists who were shut out of the event itself but who would be writing stories about it that could potentially influence public opinion.

True to journalistic form, the newspapers and television were replete with assessments of why the Clinton administration was taking on Ross Perot in a forum reminiscent of the presidential campaign's citizen debate. Some pundits attributed it to presidential weakness, and one said Clinton "cannot persuade Congress with political intimidation."[3] ABC suggested it was a strategy born of administration determination (November 4); CBS noted the advantage Gore had over Perot, someone who was less popular than the president (November 5).

Strategic musings such as these naturally evolved into predictions of how well the strategy would work. If there was a consensus among observers, it was that it would not work well. Republican strategist Ed Rollins told the *New York Times* that the debate was "the stupidest damn thing the White House can do. . . . Gore will give intellectual answers, and Perot will hit the emotional buttons and spit out sound bites" (November 6). In turn, *New York Times* correspondent Tom Friedman said on "Face the Nation," "It's hard to see what [the White House] can gain out of this" (November 7).

On November 9, when the main event finally arrived, media speculation and rhetoric escalated in a way that lent credibility to Jay Leno's humorous "Tonight Show" assertion that Gore and Perot should simply "fight it out on 'American Gladiators.'" "High noon at the Larry King corral," screamed *New York Newsday.* "It's the Bore vs. the Roar," quipped the *Detroit News,* in a reference to the contrasting public styles of the pedantic Gore and the outrageous Perot: "It's politics reduced to theater of the absurd." Salivated *USA Today,* it's "the juiciest piece of political theater since November 1992."

There was little suggestion that the debate was a debate at all or that the purpose of the event was to sharpen arguments for or against a measure that both sides agreed could profoundly affect the economy for years to come. Reporters inclined to cover policy as politics needed little coaxing to cover the debate as a wrestling match. But the White House hardly coaxed, advancing the debate idea not as high-minded discourse but as an opportunity to steal a win in the NAFTA horserace. The debate was regarded as a theatrical event by its producers and its critics. Consequently, the assumption of importance made as a matter of course about campaign debates was ironically missing—despite the fact that a major policy outcome hung in the balance and that the exchange thus was potentially more consequential than its ostensibly important but comparatively nebulous campaign cousins.

Once the event was over, news coverage followed a pattern familiar to anyone who had witnessed postgame analysis of campaign debates: Commentators applied political criteria to assess "winners" and "losers," emphasized the entertainment value of the debate, and focused on the personalities involved. ABC's "Nightline" reported the results of an instant public opinion poll on who had "won" the debate (the result: Gore by 14 percentage points). The following morning, as Gore and Perot appeared on the early network news programs to put their spin on the results, NBC's "Today" show hosted political panelists who scored the debate as if it were a boxing match. They gave the win to Gore "on points," observing that the vice president (contrary to predebate conventional wisdom) had Perot "on the ropes most of the night."

Columnists and reporters noted the utility of the debate as a popular culture television event, worthy for its entertainment value. The *Chicago Tribune* equated it with the programming available on other channels: "If you watched 'Roseanne' or 'Die-Hard 2' Tuesday night, you missed the equally entertaining and probably equally unenlightening Al and Ross show" (November 10). *New York Newsday* portrayed the debate as a mixture of campaign politics, talk radio, and situation comedy (November 11). ABC news reporter Chris Bury offered what could be seen as a predictable evaluation of his colleagues' efforts: "For all the hyperbole and handicapping, tonight's bally-hooed debate probably generated more heat than light."

The orgy of postdebate analysis continued through the next evening's network news programs. By this point, commentators were already talking about the fact that they had spent the entire day talking about the debate. Peter Jennings told his ABC viewers, "Most Americans did not see Al Gore and Ross Perot snipe and snap at each other for an hour and a half, but lots of folks are talking about it today" (November 10). In his postdebate assessment on November 11, the *Washington Post*'s David Broder may have unintentionally offered the most accurate post-mortem on all this verbiage. Pointing out how the debate had fallen short of the sort of "reasoned political discourse" imagined by the founding fathers, Broder said Gore had achieved a Pyrrhic victory. "What does it matter," he asked, "if the overwhelming impression left with viewers is that both sides are cynically disregarding the nation's good for their own selfish purposes—and subverting government in the process?"

Like debate coverage, stories about governance will at times borrow from another familiar campaign topic: personal scandal. Just like the Gennifer Flowers and draft evasion allegations covered by the press as a threat to candidate Clinton's presidential prospects, scandalous stories about possible impropriety by President Clinton and Hillary Rodham Clinton in the Whitewater real estate deal dominated media coverage during the spring of 1994. In the same way campaign scandals were framed as a threat to Clinton's candidacy, the Whitewater matter was reported as a story that could potentially dislodge the Clinton health care initiative.

Coverage focused on personality and strategy, as had news of the campaign scandals. Whitewater stories centered on issues of individual credibility, personalizing governance by drawing attention to the behavior of key political figures while emphasizing how the scandal was, in the words of one CBS report, "a constant, draining distraction" to a White House otherwise focused on health care reform (March 23, 1994). In this instance, with Hillary Rodham Clinton at the forefront of the health care effort and integrally involved in the Whitewater affair, stories that in other instances might have emphasized the president instead focused on her.

But the nature of those stories was the same and could have been mistaken for election news. Looking for an easy handle on her personality and faced with uneasy contradictions from the glowing press coverage Hillary Rodham Clinton had received the previous year, reporters set out to characterize the woman who now seemed to be hiding information and avoiding the press. Comparisons were drawn to other notable women cast darkly by the media. "She's either got to be Tonya or Nancy," said one press observer, invoking the battery of Nancy Kerrigan by agents of her Olympic skating rival Tonya Harding (Sally Quinn on CNBC, March 9). Another said she was "starting to resemble an Ozark Leona Helmsley," the imprisoned hotel magnate (*New York Post,* March 10).

Naturally, this led to public speculation about why Clinton was being secretive with the press, although reporters could have found the answer in their own feeding frenzy. There was talk of her "obsessive" distrust of the press (*Newsweek,* March 14) and of a Nixon-style breakdown in press relations (*New York Times,* March 10). The consequences of such distance were swift, strong, and equally public. "Glowing reviews have come to an end," judged the *Washington Post* (March 7). "Her once dazzling image is now tarnished," echoed CBS news (March 4).

Against this backdrop, both Clintons invested tremendous energy to get reporters to rediscover their health care proposal—an effort akin to (and as unsuccessful as) candidate Clinton trying to convince reporters they should be talking about his economic proposals rather than his sexual history. Even though, as one report noted, "most people care less about Whitewater than health care" (*Dallas Morning News,* April 7), for a period in spring 1994, coverage emphasized how the Clintons were unsuccessfully trying to shift the media focus to their policy agenda—an assertion validated each time it was made. Said CBS news, "Hillary Clinton seemed determined to let nothing shake her focus on health care, but the Whitewater controversy was never far away" (March 14). The *Los Angeles Times* reiterated that Mrs. Clinton, "even this far from Washington [at a health care event in Colorado], could not escape jarring reminders of the Whitewater controversy" (March 15). Accordingly, as ABC dutifully and reflexively reported, she "seemed to ridicule the press for making much of what was a financial investment gone bad" (March 14).

As in campaigns, when governance competes with scandal, scandal wins. And the two will compete, which ultimately is more significant than the open question of how important it is for the press to cover the questionable behavior of public officials. Critics have argued compellingly that there is a place for the latter. But government goes on regardless of the real or possible sins of its officials, whereas news coverage of government stops. The media are wont to cover policymaking as politics, and if the scandal-induced frenzy isn't enough to divert media attention from governance, the inevitable administration efforts to shift press attention to politically favorable ground is. Once this happens, policy coverage is no longer regarded as a press function by either side but as a coveted objective for the administration in a contest with the press that the latter has no intention of losing. We are left to hear about the struggle even as reporters tell us they realize we are probably more interested in other things.

This is not to say that press coverage should depoliticize governance. That would be foolhardy, because politics and governance are inseparable. But they are not identical; how they are covered makes it difficult to recognize this. Just as campaigns are not war, governance is not just a campaign: More is at stake than who is up and down in Washington. Overpoliticizing policy coverage turns the process on its head, fashioning the means to an objective as an end in its own right. Unfortunately for the viewer seeking information without an attitude, this is the prevailing message in media coverage of the president. As we shall see, it is also conveyed when the president is elevated in importance over the Congress, whose primary constitutional role in policymaking is subordinated to the more readily photographed chief executive.

## Congress: Gridlock Amid Posturing

Congress by design is a fragmented body that could accomplish little if not for compromise. Members with fixed, staggered terms represent diverse constituencies with divergent priorities and views. Throughout history, the great challenge to members of Congress has been to find a way to pull progress out of discord, to move the body beyond its natural inertia so that it could legislate.

Over the years, this has been accomplished through a combination of procedure and custom. Rules about **seniority,** for instance, were developed to stabilize congressional leadership. Members of the majority party with the most consecutive service on a committee would get to chair the committee; the representative of the other party with the longest consecutive tenure would be the ranking minority member. Similarly, new members of Congress were socialized to norms of appropriate behavior that had developed over time to facilitate the effectiveness of the institution. New members were expected to sit silently on committees and regard their more senior colleagues with deference. Visibility and leadership roles would come with service, but first-term members were expected initially to serve an informal period of **apprenticeship,** during which they were to learn the ways of Congress through quiet observation of their established peers. Senior members enforced this norm on junior members who, upon gaining seniority, would perpetuate it by imposing it on their juniors (Ripley, 1983).

During the long period while such procedures and norms were in effect, the legislative branch operated as what congressional scholar Norman Ornstein calls a **"closed system."** In short, the institution functioned essentially without public scrutiny. Although party chiefs could never dictate how to vote, power was nonetheless an internal matter, emanating from senior members in leadership positions. Legislation was written primarily in committee under the direction of committee chairs; floor votes were largely private, unrecorded matters where leaders rather than constituents kept score. The national media took little notice of the inner workings of Congress, which gave the leadership leeway to resolve differences in relative obscurity (Ornstein, 1983; Ranney, 1983).

By the late 1970s things had changed. With the expansion of network news programs to thirty minutes in the 1960s, television tapped Washington as a natural source of information about government. This spearheaded the discovery of Congress by the national media, and although legislative reporting was still secondary to presidential coverage, the preponderance of attention focused on the federal government enveloped the legislative branch as well. The introduction of cameras to the floor of the House in the late 1970s and to the Senate in the mid-1980s, as noted in Chapter 2, gave television networks the pictures they needed to make Congress a regular presence on the evening news.

After the Vietnam War and Watergate, government reformers pledging institutional change emerged in large numbers. Many were elected to Congress and began to modify some of the old procedures. As with party reform, congressional reform resulted in a more decentralized process at the expense of elite control. Partly because of party reform, members now found themselves beholden more to the interest groups that funded their campaigns than to congressional leadership divided along party lines. Being a nonconformist became easy; in fact, it became the norm (Ornstein, 1983; Mayhew, 1975).

Old procedures like the seniority system yielded to modifications enabling more junior members to attain powerful committee and subcommittee chairs. "Sunshine laws" requiring recorded floor votes made members less beholden to leadership and increased public posturing and maneuvering for the folks back home who could now track their member's record. Members, even new ones, were entitled to large staffs capable of making members more self-sufficient and less dependent on congressional leaders (Polsby, 1983). Old norms like apprenticeship, unenforceable under the glare of the television camera, rapidly slipped away. Congress had become, in Ornstein's words, an **"open system,"** visible to the public through the media and operating under the gaze of its constituents.

The new atmosphere dramatically changed how members acted. As rock-solid centers of power melted under the light of public scrutiny, Congress became an institution of individualists. Once-predictable methods of congressional self-monitoring became problematic (Barilleaux, 1988). Internal disagreements were less readily resolved by leaders who held limited sway over the rank and file. Reflecting a post-Watergate mistrust of authority, members did not fear leadership as they once had and came to see themselves as autonomous actors. There was less reason to compromise but more reason to posture for constituents. Grandstanding, even among junior members, became a regular occurrence. C-SPAN made

Contemporary legislative leaders like Newt Gingrich aggressively play to cameras and re-porters, giving Congress greater visibility than it had in past generations. New media, like C-SPAN, also heighten the exposure of Congress and other-than-presidential political actors and processes. Photo courtesy Kathleen R. Beall.

possible private home viewing of floor action. And virtually any member could now trot out a sound bite for the ever-ready, ever-hungry television camera.

According to Ornstein, members could pursue three strategies to win media attention: "become a victim of a scandal, defy conventional wisdom and conduct, or publicize an issue" (Ornstein, 1983: p. 201). The first of these occurs from time to time and obviously is not a choice media strategy for an ambitious representative.[4] The second is a favorite of members who fashion themselves as mavericks. The third—publicize an issue—is available to any member at virtually every turn. Reporters subsequently find a context for their remarks, generally emphasizing the conflict underlying what members of Congress have to say.

This is easy to do. Against the disheveled backdrop of the open system, turmoil and trouble are readily found. The dissension is often real because the mechanisms designed to bring Congress to order are far less available than they were a generation ago. When disagreement appears in the news, however, it is inevitably portrayed as problematic rather than derivative of a complex, unkempt system. When friction results, the media dutifully report it as a sign that things are malfunctioning. Viewers and readers learn of the political infighting and institutional disharmony of a body we are to assume should behave more suitably—even though by design it is decentralized and prone to protracted disagreement. If Congress is portrayed as a junior member of the federal partnership, it is seen as no less politically motivated than the presidency. Politics is once again a problem, not a description.

The media intone the term *gridlock* not as if it described a natural or expected consequence of the system but as if it were a degenerative disease. This tendency is particularly pronounced in press coverage of health care reform, an undertaking so massive that nonincremental congressional action would have to be considered remarkable. Still, day after day, Congress is said to be mired in the details of several competitive proposals, unable to move swiftly. Sometimes, particularly in the print media or on C-SPAN, the details of those measures are presented, without comment, for the reader or viewer to study and absorb. More likely, as was often the case with health care reform, coverage emphasizes events rather than ideas, and the frame of reference for understanding the action is the knockdown politics of a hardball campaign.

A committee debate is described as "unusually divisive" by the *New York Times.*[5] Republicans and Democrats are "as defiantly divided as ever," claims a *Dallas Morning News* report, "scolding one another for the reform jam in Congress." Members posture against members, partisans all. "The crabbing in the Ways and Means Committee was one-sided," adds the *Times,* "as one [Republican] after another complained at being excluded." Not surprisingly, "the prospects of bipartisanship seemed dim."

This NBC report portrayed congressional backbiting in the most personal of terms:

> Behind the scenes, the infighting among Senate Democrats is fierce. Democratic senators told NBC News that the president's key allies [Senate Majority Leader George Mitchell and West Virginia Senator Jay Rockefeller] are actively undermining [Senate Finance Committee Chairman Daniel Patrick Moynihan], saying he's too eager to compromise with Republicans. Both Mitchell and Rockefeller deny the charge. Another Clinton ally said the president is also exasperated because Moynihan "won't shut up." The relations between the two men aren't good. . . . Key [Democrats] warn that undercutting Moynihan could destroy chances for health reform this year (May 18, 1994).

Electoral politics, rather than ideological disagreement, is a favorite explanation for why Congress fails to act. Often an apt interpretation, it is but one reason for institutional division. Nonetheless, a struggle among Democrats to agree on health care funding is said to derive not from different economic assumptions about the effect of requiring small businesses to insure their employees but from concerns about political survival. "The problem," said Chris Bury of ABC, "is [1994] is an election year and congressmen know the paradox they face—the desire of Americans for health reform has yet to be matched by their appetite to pay for it" (April 28, 1994). In a similar vein, divisions among Republicans are explained not in terms of philosophical questions about the advisability of price controls or the possible consequences of employer mandates but in the language of political costs: "[Republican] leaders like [Senate Minority Leader Robert] Dole and [House Republican Whip] Newt Gingrich are convinced the party courts disaster at the polls if it looks too hard-line on health care" (ABC, "World News Tonight," March 3, 1994).

The prevailing assumption behind congressional coverage is that somehow, amid the partisan wrangling, the legislative branch is expected to act on policy questions. Accordingly, time becomes an important part of the story. NBC announced in late spring 1994 that "[Senator Edward M.] Kennedy promised that his Labor Committee would produce a bill within ten days" (May 18). The *Washington Post* noted that "so much is at stake in the health care debate" for congressional Democrats "that leaders in both chambers are going to extraordinary lengths to convince the public that a bill will be churned out by the end of the 103rd Congress" (May 19).

This effort occurred in the wake of the political rhetoric of 1992, which promised massive, imminent health care reform and thereby set high performance expectations for Congress and the Clinton presidency. Of course, a legislative effort as monstrous as health reform is going to generate congressional acrimony and division. But the promise of action became the readily accepted expectation against which reporters evaluated the legislative process. Disagreements ranging from partisan to personal became benchmarks for measuring the congressional drive toward the goal and were interpreted as if they were lost yardage in a football game—as unfortunate movement in the wrong direction.

Bickering thus becomes a symbol of how Congress is failing to work rather than a predictable (and not always significant) by-product of how Congress works. No matter that Congress has wrestled unsuccessfully with health care for over fifty years, or that members began debate divided over diverse, irreconcilable solutions. Improvements in health care were promised by politicians. Obstacles to that goal would be viewed by the media as a failure of the legislature to act and the inability of the president to fulfill a campaign pledge, not as the natural product of a decentralized system.

As we have seen, presidents attempt to keep their word, even when what they promise is beyond their institutional ability to deliver. Similarly, good-faith policy differences underlie much congressional posturing. But this interpretation of events is hard to come by. Instead, both institutions are forced to operate amid intensely politicized interpretations of their behavior and unrealistic expectations for action perpetuated by how the media portray governance. If Clinton's promise of health care reform was grandiose, it was also inevitable given how the system is supposed to function. Would-be presidents need to appear ready to impose their way on a Congress that should move swiftly and collectively to address national problems. If any readers become skeptical that major reforms will happen, it is probably not because they believe Congress is designed to move slowly and frustrate initiative but because they have learned that Congress and the president could have moved on something but fell victim to political infighting. If inaction ultimately leads the reader to disappointment, this is a reasonable reaction to the media frame.

## Interest Groups: Bargaining for Self-Gain

Whereas news coverage plays on erroneous expectations of legislative behavior, it portrays interest groups in a narrow manner bordering on caricature. In the press, interest groups are presented as pressure-generating organizations staffed by well-paid professionals who extract goodies from the public sector for the benefit of a choice constituency. Perhaps this is a valid way to characterize some groups. But it is not the only way, nor is it universally applicable. The media less readily apply the label "interest group" to activities that are not manipulative or to groups that serve the needs of resource-poor individuals, just as they tend not to suggest that interests could play an important representative function.

Interest groups as a source of news receive far less attention than the president and his administration—one-third as much, according to one recent count (Danielian and Page, 1994). When they are portrayed in the media, "interest groups" are typically addressed in terms of conflict. They are identified with lobbying activities, which connote coercion, even though interests frequently engage in activities that would not be classified as lobbying, and much lobbying is cooperative, not combative. This portrayal is consistent with the governance-as-horserace frame. **Lobbyists** are cast as dastardly supporting players who complicate the system as they work it, ensuring that whatever emerges from the legislative process will satisfy the varied piecemeal concerns of vaguely labeled "special interests."

It is a convincing portrayal for many people, given that according to one practitioner, "Being a lobbyist has long been synonymous in the minds of many Americans with being a glorified pimp" (Birnbaum, 1992: p. 7). This impression masks the complexity of the lobbying effort and the background as well as the behavior of those who practice it. Media coverage evokes images of the back-slapping, cigar-smoking, arm-twisting, smooth-talking lobbyist of myth and, on occasion, reality. "But right behind those classic types of lobbyists," claims scholar Jeffrey Birnbaum, "are people with more targeted and potentially more potent sales skills: economists, lawyers, direct-mail and telephone salespeople, public-relations experts, pollsters, economists, and even accountants" (Birnbaum, 1992: pp. 5–6). Many do not engage in direct lobbying of representatives at all, instead using their resources to mobilize their constituents or make mediated appeals like the "Harry and Louise" ads discussed in Chapter 2 (Walker, 1991).

These professionals play a role in lobbying because lobbying is as much about information as it is about arm-twisting. Other perspectives on lobbying emphasize the service interest groups provide members of Congress by supplying them with technical information on specialized aspects of legislation or with political information about where other members stand on matters under discussion—information that facilitates intelligent decisionmaking in the face of great time constraints. This perspective features the mutual interests shared by members of Congress and lobbyists and suggests a more positive view of the lobbying enterprise than implied by the "pressure" label (Truman, 1955).

In this regard, lobbyists can be understood to perform an important representative role for members of the public who find their interests expressed through organized groups. This perspective emphasizes flexibility by lobbyists, rather than unyielding, heavy-handed tactics, and conciliation toward representatives, with whom compromises are often more viable than threats. The public interest, in this view, is well served by the actions of groups that operate on behalf of their constituents (Berry, 1984).

Whether this desirable effect is actually achieved is, of course, debatable. It is an open and important question whether the legislative process effectively manages the conflicting demands of interest groups such that more groups mean representation for more people, or whether the system is hijacked by the sheer number of groups with access to it (Berry, 1984; Lowi, 1969; Truman, 1955). But the media do not raise this question because they believe the verdict is already in—if not on the system, then on the people who operate within it. Interests—more specifically, lobbies—are treated pejoratively, their actions viewed as problematic rather than predictable components of a system that, for better or worse, operates on the principle of organized access. The process is simplified while the players are vilified.

Consider again the case of HIAA and its "Harry and Louise" commercials. When President Clinton and his allies derided the ad campaign as an attempt by a "pressure group" to undermine his health care reform efforts, he characterized the organization in a manner readily identifiable to reporters. This offered the press an accessible frame for portraying the comments and assured that the president's perspective on the ad campaign would take hold in the news. When President Clinton overrepresented the objective of the ads (as we noted in Chapter 2, HIAA sought to modify, not undermine, the White House proposal), Clinton's accusations rather than the actual intent of the ad campaign became the standard for coverage. Reporters did not challenge the president's interpretation of the ads on the basis of their understanding of what Harry and Louise were saying, as reporters sometimes do when they believe the statements of public officials are at odds with the record.

Like the organizations they represent, individuals functioning as lobbyists are readily portrayed in terms of the manipulative functions they perform. Even Ross Perot was treated as a lobbyist, albeit a high-profile one, during the waning days of the NAFTA deliberations. As he went "office-to-office, trailed by fans like a rock star" (*USA Today,* November 11, 1993), he engaged in the usual combative activities of the newspaper version of a lobbyist, "buttonholing close to 100 representatives, working the phones, . . . padding the marble halls relentlessly in search of votes" (*New York Times,* November 17). Moreover, while Perot was out working the legislators and the cameras, the real dirty work was being done in his name by a man the *Wall Street Journal* called a textile "tycoon," Roger Milliken. According to the *Journal,* Perot's obviously wealthy partner worked stealthily behind the scenes, content to let Perot "do the roaring—while he, much less conspicuously, underwrites a sub rosa lobbying machine that has been working for months to kill the pact" (November 15). Implicit in this account are the deceit and power behind the real lobbying effort: an organized, furtive, well-financed policy-killing machine operating in the shadows.

By emphasizing congressional and presidential capitulation to interest group demands, the media underscore this heavy-handed perspective and lend credibility to the notion that lobbyists strong-arm legislators. During the NAFTA deliberations, ABC noted how President Clinton had succumbed to interest-group pressure to drop proposed grazing fee increases from consideration, thereby winning ten Republican votes for the treaty. "That's something the [NAFTA] opponents simply can't match," ABC reported (November 9). One day later, the *Journal of Commerce* commented on efforts by textile manufacturers who used "the horse-trading of congressional votes [over NAFTA] to push for smaller cuts in U.S. tariffs in world trade negotiations."

Perhaps the term "horsetrading" best characterizes the media perspective on interest-group activity. The tactic involves the key players in the media version of governance—the president, Congress, and interest groups—coming together in a shrewd, cynical way to make policy by in effect giving away the public trust. "Congress for sale," shouted the brassy *New York Post* over legislative capitulation to supposed interest-group demands (November 17). Said the more mainstream Tom Brokaw, "President Clinton has done everything but offer the White House for get-away weekends to congressmen undecided on NAFTA" (November 16).

But the "wheeling and dealing" (ABC, "World News Tonight," November 16) is also "business as usual" (NBC, "Today," November 17). It may be "squalid, seedy . . . vote-buying" to conservative commentator Pat Buchanan appearing on ABC's "Good Morning America" (November 17), yet that evening, on the same network, viewers were told that "Mr. Clinton is hardly the first president to engage in horse-trading when facing defeat on a major issue." The combined message is that the behavior is both unsavory and ordinary—reprehensible, perhaps, but unavoidable.

Something resembling horsetrading, of course, does occur in democratic systems. But to characterize the actions of interest groups and policymakers in the language of quid pro quo is to portray as unwholesome a process that could not operate without self-interest. Some lobbyists saw an opening in the contentious NAFTA battle and tried to get whatever they could; some legislators maximized the trade value of their votes. But we could also say these individuals were representing their constituents, just as there were participants who cared about the implications of the trade pact and acted according to their beliefs. In media coverage, this perspective is harder to find.

The following comment, made in late 1993 by a CNN reporter, is far more typical. In assessing Hillary Rodham Clinton's attack on the insurance industry as an opponent of health care, Bruce Morton said, "It won't do her any harm at all with the public. Now, it may annoy some lobbyists. The lobbyists may influence a congressman or two. You know, people don't like the insurance industry any more than people like most big things. And if you go after them, you're wearing a populist hat and you tend to look pretty good" (November 7).

Morton just as readily could have been talking about himself.


## Conclusion

We need to be provided with adequate information not only to offer sensible feedback about the policies we want government to pursue but also to make informed judgments on election day about how well elected officials have performed their jobs. Unfortunately, the information about governance provided on television and in print is often cloudy. Coverage is replete with erroneous or misleading assumptions about the system, and it is difficult to learn enough about what is going on to draw intelligent conclusions about policy development, no less to feel as if one's conclusions could make a difference.

What is the reader or viewer to make of governance given the way it is portrayed by the media? Regardless of the details of a particular policy or program, it is easy to conclude that policymaking is simply politics in the pejorative sense. The truthful assertion that no people can govern themselves without politics is distorted by a mediated framework that paints governance in the lowest possible partisan terms; the conclusion suggested is that self-gain repeatedly edges out the collective good. Interest groups act aggressively to protect their turf. Members of Congress fret about the next election. Presidents worry about themselves and calculate each move according to probabilistic estimates of how to increase their popularity. Self-absorbed reporters tell us about everyone else's selfishness. From this self-feeding process, we somehow govern ourselves.

Some people might think there is a grain of truth in this characterization of Washington. Perhaps there is. If the media simply disparaged the motives of the primitive life forms in the primordial soup, we could possibly get by, finding meaning amid the nonsense and filtering out the noise. But the media do more, relating details of the system as it looks to the media, which is to say with television rather than the Constitution at the center. They inexorably distort the roles played by the principal participants and turn realistic performance expectations upside down.

The media have it all wrong. They cover governance as if we had a presidential system, as if the chief executive really did outweigh Congress. They elevate the president to impossible heights, then tear him down when he turns out to be unable to perform beyond his constitutional capability. They personalize the office, equating the president's individual triumphs with an odd sort of national success, then undermine the progress of his legislative agenda when his real or alleged sins show him to be a flawed sovereign. The president plays to this media frame, raising expectations with promises of performance, then tries to circumvent reporters with televised media events offering the illusion of direct public participation. Dutifully, reporters cover his actions and raise doubts about his motives.

As for Congress, the media tell us that body is subordinate to the president, a foot-dragging institution not readily given a telegenic human face. Gridlock is portrayed as a systemic abnormality rather than as a hallmark of the separation of powers, something from which only the Herculean president can rescue us—if he is as good as his rhetoric, which of course he rarely is. Perhaps, it is suggested, Congress would be a better place if it stood up to interest groups more and the president less, even though the former maintain mutually beneficial relationships with members far more naturally than does the latter.

The media provide us with a sharp picture of how government works. Nevertheless, it is their picture, real to the reporters who live it but misleading for the audience. As mediated reality, judgments about what matters are made according to criteria that concern the press. Thus we learn that a president wished to talk about a policy initiative, but reporters knew better than to let him deflect attention from news of his latest indiscretion. We learn how critical it is to his political fortunes that Congress approve health care reform before the next election. We learn that he promised to end legislative gridlock in the last election, but Congress still speaks with hundreds of voices, posing yet another political quagmire.

Somehow, some of the time, policy emerges from all this. To determine whether it is responsible or good policy requires a basis for assessing what government does beyond the image manipulation and political posturing emphasized in mediated accounts of governance. This informed view is hard to achieve, which makes it difficult for us to take an active role in governing ourselves should we still wish to after consuming so much dreadful information about the system.

The scholar Ryan Barilleaux identifies this as a problem of evaluation. In comments specifically about the president, he argues that television makes the chief executive simultaneously more visible and more distant. Through television, we gain tremendous exposure to the president, but the emphasis on posturing, winning, and success provides little of value for us to determine intelligently if in fact we like what we see. He identifies this as a "double bind" for presidents—and citizens:

> The president is evaluated on the basis of outcomes, but voters do not receive a neutral picture of presidential reality from television. So, the president takes measures to secure favorable media coverage, but in doing so interferes with effective public evaluation of his performance in office. Even without adopting the cynical view that no president wants accurate evaluations, only good evaluations, no one can say that the public interest is served by this situation (Barilleaux, 1988: p. 138).

The same could be said of other actors in the system and of the entire process of governance. When we cannot accurately evaluate the actions of our political leaders, we cannot make good decisions for ourselves. Should we decide not to try, we forfeit one of our most important public responsibilities.

Media coverage of governance makes good evaluation difficult because it makes the overall effort less appealing. Even for those motivated to learn about the public realm, it is hard to come by information that is not structured by the partisan, political assumptions of the media frame. Whether there is recourse for the dedicated and choice for the rest will be considered in the final chapter.

# 5

.......................................................................................

# What About Us?

TV cameramen filmed print reporters, who were
listening to White House officials, who were being
interviewed by talk show hosts, who were fielding
telephone calls from people around the country. . . .
Clintonites dubbed the event as an act of public
relations genius.

—*New York Newsday,*
September 24, 1993

W<small>HAT IS GOING ON HERE</small>? Presidential media strategists converted the White House into a satellite-link bazaar so that talk show hosts, awed by the setting, would pipe sympathetic messages about the Clinton health care proposal to home audience participants. Newspaper reporters covered the action and became part of the story told to evening news viewers on television; even that fact was subsequently reported in the newspaper account reprinted above. Administration officials called it an act of genius. Others may not be so sure.

What is going on is the marketing of the presidency by aides and the deconstruction of politics by reporters, all of whom are part of a system that thrives on turning the political process inside out. Politicians and their handlers seek advantage in the vast information capabilities provided by emerging and existent media technology, applying the age-old need for agenda control to contemporary media realities. So they hold new and creative media events like the call-in stunt on the White House lawn, knowing they are sure to get a double publicity bang for their investment by reaching people directly on the talk shows and indirectly through subsequent media coverage. Reporters predictably show up but cover the meaning and purpose behind the event rather than simply the fact that it was held. In essence, they tell us what the handlers already know—that it was a stunt—and thus reveal in their account of events the manipulative heart of politics.

Coverage like this divulges the guts of a system in which both reporters and politicians have a vested interest. Such stories make good copy by giving the reporter a superior perch from which to chirp about the manipulative ways of others—a "gotcha" story without the sex. Politicians benefit because they get their message in the news. It doesn't matter if the words are unflattering because people will remember the pictures.

But what about us? We see the pictures—and we get the message: Our political process is populated with devious handlers who try to orchestrate our opinions and regulate our affections. And perhaps it is. Taken judiciously, this sort of coverage provides a real service. Repeated daily, there may be side effects.

The message undermines the very things that information is supposed to facilitate in a democracy; it renders political accountability and public participation problematic. We learn about health care as we look deep into the dark heart of those who would have our attention for a fleeting moment, long enough to internalize the

White House line of the day. If governance is all just a show, where is the commitment of its producers, save to the momentary gain in public support they seek for their administration? When public opinion pollsters register fickle shifts in public passions, would officials not pitch their tent on other ground, spinning for reporters a new line for another day? Today health care, tomorrow foreign policy. A new issue, a new media event, but no continuity and certainly no courage.

Instead of an inclusive dialogue with politicians and officials, we get an advanced lesson in public relations. Instead of feeling energized by the efforts of political leaders or drawn to the fortitude of the guardian press, we experience everyone in the same dirty puddle, mud wrestling. Reporters may believe they are above the fray, but when they acknowledge their struggle with political manipulators, they are in fact engaging in reciprocal manipulation. We see them on the White House lawn, too, cameras in hand, guardians of the faith who would drop anything for an invitation to a state dinner with those they supposedly revile. Seeing through the pretext is not hard. Finding reason to participate in a system like this is.

News stories of this variety provide little in the way of useful, alternative political information that might combat messages about how politics is conducted. Outside the analyses, the sound bites of which reporters speak provide the greatest competition for our attention. But these are hardly a sound basis for reasoned political thought. Condensed to five-second blurbs, political messages become little more than disparate slogans, difficult to assimilate and connect, appropriate for little more than the most simplistic decisionmaking. Alone, they would make no sense at all; embedded in the thematic message of the story, they are supporting footnotes for the reporter's analysis of political gamesmanship (Stuckey, 1991; Polsby and Wildavsky, 1980).

## Real Variety or More of the Same?

As we know, there are venues other than television and newspaper stories for learning about politics. Reporters keep telling us we live in the information age, which means we are not bound to listen exclusively to them. Given the variety of media we discussed in Chapter 1, it would appear that somewhere we should be able to find sources of material to foster intelligent participation and make government less repulsive.

Perhaps we can—but we need to be motivated enough to seek different perspectives and savvy enough to interpret what we find. Two possibilities are the Internet and media outside the ideological center. The first of these is new and emerging, the second old and staid. Computers offer the promise of everything from raw data on legislative voting records to hard news to political gossip. Magazines of the right and left promise just the opposite—opinion and interpretation—but with clearly defined ideological slants that separate them from the popular press.

Both the Internet and ideological media are problematic as alternative sources of information. There is a massive amount of material available on-line—but that is the Internet's biggest problem. Apart from the effort required to swim through oceans of political material, it takes a discriminating eye to separate hard news from opinions—or lies. And, the Internet is loaded with both. Unsubstantiated rumors thrive on the Net about everything from the circumstances surrounding the death of White House aide Vincent Foster to the personal lives of the president and first lady. Without journalists to guide us away from the most blatantly misleading information, it is hard to separate facts from convincing-looking fiction. Ironically, computer networks offer us an escape from the stifling frames of mainstream reporting, but as a forum where anybody with an on-line computer can say anything she wants, the Internet offers too much freedom to be a reliable alternative to mainstream news.

Publications that disseminate ideas outside the political center are also problematic. Like Internet users, those receptive to ideas at or past the edges of the political mainstream need motivation to find them. Although some are no doubt motivated to seek views other than their own in the pursuit of political learning, media appealing to the left and right of the political spectrum will most naturally reach those already there. Like the party press of old, these media speak to the converted. They offer different approaches to politics than their mainstream counterparts, but they are not likely choices for the mass audience.

Beyond possibilities like these, genuine alternatives are few, despite the appearance of tremendous choice. Such options as televised "town meetings," radio and telephone talk shows, cable news, and even tabloid media share dynamics with each other and with conventional reporting that make them more likely to reinforce than challenge the messages we get elsewhere.

On the surface, interactive events like televised "town meetings" provide an opportunity for the exchange of information on a large scale. They may be reduced to stories about political strategy on the evening news, but live on television they promise direct access to public officials and something resembling participatory democracy in its pure form.

Unfortunately, this appearance is an illusion. Real town meetings are exercises in planning and decisionmaking. Held in small communities and in face-to-face settings, they provide participants with the opportunity to share their ideas with others and modify their positions for the greater good of consensus building. Decisions can be made, and citizens can feel as if they have a say in the outcome, even if their position does not win the day.

Televised town meetings permit none of this. The "global village" is not a large-scale version of the New England town but an electronically linked zone where many people who do not know each other can have the same private experience simultaneously. Television viewing is a passive diversion, something we can do while cradling a beer. Involvement in politics is an active enterprise, something we do with our neighbors.[1] The two do not mix very well.

Few people actually participate in televised events. For most of us, our role is vicarious: We shake our heads in disagreement with an answer or mutter how a question is much like one we would have asked. But we do not interact or even interface; we simply watch. This experience may be engrossing, but it more resembles voyeuristic entertainment than political involvement.

The few who do speak to the president (or assembled public figures) rarely have the opportunity to ask follow-up questions. Citizens are not journalists; they are not particularly skilled at generating the sort of responsible, high-level discourse that could lead to reasoned discussion of important matters (Jamieson, 1992). This limits real debate and results in an exchange of words that assumes the rhetorical form reporters decry when they speak of the manipulative efforts of politicians. Jeffrey Tulis has examined the format:

> Constitutional government, which was established in contradistinction to government by assembly, now has become a kind of government by assembly without a genuine assembling of people. In this fictive assembly, television speaks to the president in metaphors expressive of the "opinions" of a fictive people, and the president responds to the demands and words created by the media with rhetoric designed to manipulate popular passions rather than to engage citizens in political debate (Tulis, 1987: p. 188).

In other words, town meetings put us inside the sound bites. They substitute the appearance of access for the real thing, doing more harm than good for those who believe them to be an adequate substitute for other forms of political participation. Since their fundamental premise—that they are participatory events—is false, they readily reinforce the cynical incantations about politics heard elsewhere in the media. The viewer is invited to share the deceit and momentarily feel the ambiance of a New England town hall, but if the feeling doesn't last beyond the first ten minutes of "ER," it is because the televised "meeting" hardly qualifies as a real alternative.

Other options, although popular, fare little better. Talk radio, for instance, has grown steadily in popularity over the past decade; by one estimate, it is heard by at least 15 million people daily (Owen, 1993). The same study finds this audience to be a demographically diverse group of patrons from across the ideological spectrum, and although conservative hosts like Rush Limbaugh talk the loudest and get the most attention, listeners are united as much by disaffection from government as by partisan beliefs. This last point is important because it suggests that talk radio reaches people longing for a say in a political process dominated by large institutions and distant voices. Listeners tune in for political discussion on a human scale.

What they get could be more aptly described as catharsis than dialogue. Although more telephone calls are answered on talk radio than on town meeting broadcasts, the two venues are otherwise quite similar. Both lack purposeful discussion and a way for callers to interact meaningfully with guests, who are often pundits or academics selling a book or politicians or handlers spinning their political line. Larry King refrains from tough follow-up questions of guests, who appear agenda in hand. Rush Limbaugh makes strong allegations in flamboyant language against people and policies he dislikes. None of this constitutes high-level discourse.

Because some people get through, talk radio creates the semblance of a connection to the political world, and listeners are left with the feeling that their voice is being heard. This is an important contribution. But it is not a substitute for being connected to the political world, which requires more than simply listening or viewing. Ironically, the inability of listeners to transcend the limits of the medium leaves talk radio to perpetuate the very need it appears to fulfill; it keeps people hooked on its personalities and guests and ensures they come back for more.

For different reasons, the ever-present watchfulness of cable news and the highly regarded (in academic circles) offerings of public broadcasting fall short of qualifying as alternatives to mainstream media. In terms of content, CNN and PBS have taken something less than what political analyst Martin Schram describes as a "major stride towards expanding the scope and depth of the news that is available throughout America" (Schram, 1987: p. 18). Whereas CNN offers convenience and PBS does, in fact, permit greater depth, both services feature the same political suspects talking about politics in essentially the same way as in other media reports.

In the 1980s, CNN indeed seemed promising: "The Cable News Network greatly expanded television's ability to serve as a purveyor of nonstop news. At all hours, CNN provides viewers with news that is as up-to-date and complete as ABC, CBS, or NBC provide at their morning, noon, and nighttime public feeding" (Schram, 1987: p. 18). This added benefit is fundamentally a matter of expedience. Insomniacs, news junkies, and instant-gratification seekers may turn to

CNN at their will for the latest stories. But they will find essentially the same version of politics available from conventional sources. In 1992, for instance, CNN differed little from its broadcast counterpart ABC in the thematic content of its election coverage. Viewers following the campaign on cable news could still conclude that it was about horserace and scandal, personality and political ambition. All that was added was the ability to hear about it at their leisure (Kerbel, 1998).

Public broadcasting, less restricted by commercial considerations, provides more details about politics and governance than most commercial news programs. But, again, this constitutes more information about the same things. Consider the following excerpts from coverage of Bill Clinton during the 1996 general election campaign. Each aired on "NewsHour with Jim Lehrer," which appears nightly on PBS:

- On press coverage of emerging details of a Clinton campaign finance scandal, presidential historian Doris Kearns Goodwin observed: "He's been around with his flaws, with his scandals, so for the press to find one of these new things—they're not going to win a Pulitzer Prize by saying the same thing that happened and has been talked about for the last four years" (October 25, 1996).
- On Clinton's character, correspondent Kwame Holman said: The scandal-plagued resignation of political assistant Dick Morris "probably doesn't help President Clinton's standing with voters on the character issue. Polls show voters still have serious questions about the president's character" (August 28, 1996).
- On Clinton in the horserace, columnist Paul Gigot noted: "Bill Clinton is all about tactics. He's all about maneuvering and slicing and making distinctions and finessing things. . . . If you're going to beat Bill Clinton, you have a strategy, you have to go right at it, you have to keep pounding away and pounding away and pounding away" (October 25, 1996).

The same set of individuals populating commercial television portray the election in the same fundamental way. Journalists in public broadcasting may also offer detailed discussion of policy issues of the sort not readily found in other sources, but they do not abandon the frame of reference that portrays politics in partisan, personal terms. The same may be said for National Public Radio (NPR), whose reporters have been heard to interpret the significance of the draft story in familiar character terms[2] or analyze the NAFTA battle as a campaign horserace.[3]

Rather than offer diversity, many of the numerous outlets providing political information reinforce each other in a perplexing blur of news, "infotainment," and advertising. Consider Box 5.1, which lists the similar themes and guests appearing on prominent news and discussion programs within a twenty-four-hour period surrounding one of the candidate debates. Cable and network television offered a continuous supply of reporters and handlers interchangeably offering their insight, first on how they predicted the debate would go, then on how they thought it had gone. The reporters appeared for ratings, the operatives for favorable spin, but the story they told was the same. If October 6 and 7 are unusual on this score, it is only in the magnitude of attention given to political news. On virtually any given night or morning, these and similar programs provide interchangeable speakers analyzing the political story of the moment from the same familiar perspective.

For another example, take the simple matter of the allegation by Gennifer Flowers that she had had an affair with Bill Clinton. Flowers came forward at a press conference sponsored by the tabloid *Star,* which featured its own promotional materials: a poster-size blowup of the paper's screaming front page. We have already seen how her claims spread like a wildfire to the quasi-mainstream *New York Post* and from there to legitimate news sources everywhere. Flowers subsequently repeated her charges on the aptly named television tabloid program "A Current Affair" in an interview previewed (and thereby promoted) in *USA Today* (February 6, 1992).

This, in turn, sparked Clinton consultant James Carville to assert that Roger Ailes, a Republican counterpart with connections to George Bush, had links to "A Current Affair"—implying a Bush connection to the Flowers allegation. Not only were the Carville assertions reported in the press,[4] but hours later on CNN, Larry King queried his guests—Democratic National Committee chairman Ron Brown and Bush Labor Secretary Lynn Martin—about their knowledge of the Ailes-"Affair" connection. This prompted an on-air telephone call from Hollywood producer and Clinton supporter Linda Bloodworth-Thomason, who insisted she knew "one hundred percent that Mr. Roger Ailes is a consultant for . . . 'A Current Affair.'" The next morning, Ailes appeared on the "Today" show, where Bryant Gumbel asserted with certainty: "The word is out that the Gennifer Flowers story was leaked by one Roger Ailes." Ailes denied the charges, suggesting they were the work of Democrats desperate for electoral success.

News blends into advertising and entertainment as readily as innuendo becomes conventional wisdom. Print and video tabloids smudge together with their more respectable cousins. Journalism becomes gossip, and politics becomes popular culture. It doesn't seem to matter where we turn.

In an interview about health care, CBS anchor Dan Rather asked Hillary Rodham Clinton, "Are you prepared to do as Vice President Al Gore did? Are you pre-

· · · · · · · · · · · · · · · · · · · · · · · · · · · · · · · · · · · · · · · · · · · · · · · · · · · · · · · · · · · · · · · · · · · · · · · · · · · · · · ·

**BOX 5.1**
**Themes and Guests Featured on Major Network**
**and Cable News Programs, October 6–7, 1996**

NBC "Meet the Press": Jack Kemp previews the upcoming debate.

CBS "Face the Nation": Professor Kathleen Hall Jamieson anticipates the impact of the upcoming debate.

FOX "News Sunday": Democratic Sen. Christopher Dodd and Republican Donald Rumsfeld discuss the upcoming debate.

CNN "World News": The lead story is about debate expectations.

NBC "Today": Clinton press secretary Mike McCurry and Dole adviser Charlie Black discuss the debate.

CBS "This Morning": Reform Party candidate Ross Perot discusses the debate.

ABC "World News Tonight": The lead story is about debate reactions.

CBS "Evening News": The lead story is about debate reactions.

NBC "Nightly News": The lead story is about debate reactions.

MSNBC "News with Brian Williams": The lead story is about debate reactions.

PBS "NewsHour": Mark Shields and Paul Gigot analyze the debate.

ABC "Nightline": Correspondents Chris Wallace, Brit Hume, John Cochran, Chris Bury, and Jeff Greenfield discuss the debate.

*Source:* Vanderbilt University Television News Archives and Burrelle's Transcripts.

pared to pay the ultimate price and go on David Letterman?" (September 22, 1993). Why *not* ask that question? The vice president *did* go on "Late Show" to publicize the administration's initiative to scale back the federal government. And it made sense. In a comical vein, late-night political humor echoes the same themes—and features the same personalities—as political reporting.

David Letterman did not dispel any of the doubts raised by media coverage when he joked, as he did in early 1992, "To stem the flow of illegal aliens coming across [from Mexico] . . . rather than spending all that money to hire [new border guards], . . . they should position someone down there to show these aliens a list of the presidential candidates" ("Late Night," February 12). Likewise, Jay Leno offered a refrain on a familiar media theme when he took on two battered political characters: "You know you're in trouble," he said of Bill Clinton, "when you make Dan Quayle's war record look good" ("Tonight Show," February 11). Cracked Dennis Miller in a somewhat sharper reference to the Vietnam and Flowers controversies, "I think it's ironic that Vietnam was the only time [Clinton] didn't see any action" ("The Dennis Miller Show," February 7).

Soft humor blends naturally with hard news because the lines between Washington and Hollywood and New York have become so thin as to make the form and content of press coverage hard to differentiate from a movie-of-the week offering. The audience can be forgiven if it has trouble distinguishing the serious business of government from the lighthearted pleasures of entertainment in an era when the White House lawn serves as a television sound stage and weighty charges are leveled at would-be presidents in tabloid papers. Reporters cap the confusion when they lend authority to the proceedings by discussing them in the news.

But trivializing politics does not reduce its importance. To the contrary, it raises the cost of governing ourselves by clouding the consequential with the inane. When political discourse mixes smoothly with social sideshow, nothing is special because everything is sensational. As if in an infinite regress, Monica Lewinsky steals the talk show stage from the late Princess Diana, who replaced O. J. Simpson, who dislodged the Whitewater scandal, which bested Tonya Harding, who displaced the Menendez brothers, who were heir apparent to Amy Fisher, who followed in the footsteps of Gennifer Flowers. And on and on: politics and celebrity; sex, violence, and elections. Nearly everywhere we turn, the message is the same.

## Incentive to Change?

It bears repeating that the political coverage we have addressed here is far more than the simple creation of the press. It is part of a system. Key players on the political scene either derive benefit from it and consequently seek to perpetuate it, or they do not gain from the system but are poorly situated to controvert it. The combined effect leaves us with meager evidence to argue that change is inevitable.

Candidates and officeholders secure short-term political gain from maneuvering the media to their agenda. Television networks, newspapers, and other media outlets reap the harvest of exciting, action-laden, visually appealing plotlines. Reporters and correspondents indulge in the ego gratification of a process that puts them on the same footing with celebrity politicians and handlers and makes them stars. Political parties and their elites, losers in a process that has shifted control of the nominating function to the mass media, are natural candidates to seek meaningful change in the system. But their potential as catalysts is limited.

Political leaders have worked for many years to develop a process by which they could manage the public agenda. The death of the partisan press, which made the task easy, ushered in a long period of tactical enhancements designed to strengthen the weak constitutional hand dealt the president. Modern media tools took the effort to a new level and, in combination with party and campaign finance reform, extended it to the electoral arena. It has been a struggle. Control is a rare commodity in an open system, and even with sophisticated opinion poll analysis and clever media events, we have seen how presidents and candidates regularly fall short of their objectives at the hands of an aggressive press.

But political figures will take what they can get, and in an era when that means being able to circumvent the press with their own shop-at-home satellite service, they get a lot. The Clintons need not come to your home and talk to you personally about health care, as Tom Brokaw mused they might. They already have your attention. Reporters may follow up by explaining the ugly details of what they had to do to get it, but that hardly matters if an additional 3 percent of us register approval for the Clinton policy in the administration's next national survey.

There are risks. Playing to the mediated myth of the strong leader who get things done means promising more than the system is designed to deliver and then being held accountable by a press corps that gleefully reruns videotape footage of specific campaign promises that do not quite mesh with performance. But the leader can always call one more press conference, hold one more town meeting, stage one more media event, and know that people will come. The stage is his until we vote him off; up to that point, it is still possible to sway a few more undecideds or shave a point or two off the percentage that think he's doing a terrible job.

This short-term strategy may pay off, although the history of the presidency in the television era suggests otherwise. Lyndon Johnson withdrew from contention in 1968 in the wake of deep national divisions over a televised war and televised domestic riots; he believed if he ran for reelection, he would fall short. Richard Nixon took methods of control to unprecedented levels, manipulating television to craft a new image for himself, only to resign his office in the wake of a scandal worthy of the old Nixon, a scandal that could not have happened in an open environment. After Watergate, Gerald Ford was voted out of office. The same fate visited Jimmy Carter and George Bush. Ronald Reagan survived two terms despite the Iran-contra scandal, although he did not leave Washington with his reputation intact. Had there been a presidential election in 1994 with Bill Clinton on the ballot, he too would have been a likely candidate for early retirement. Clinton survived to win reelection in 1996, but, as in 1992, a majority of voters supported someone else.

Despite the poor odds, presidents keep at it. All of these men experienced some victories along the way, some short-term boosts that must have led them to believe that, in their case, it would be different. They keep playing the game, perhaps believing that different rules requiring greater accountability would actually be worse. It is hard to see how it would be worse for the nation, but in the short term, which is how politics is played, it could make things harder for the strategists. Thus there is little incentive to change.

But shortsightedness overlooks the systemic malady reflected in our recent history of disposable presidents. We keep changing our leaders, looking for something we are continually promised but cannot find, because the process, as Schram says, is cynical. It is hard for us to believe that people are drawn to public service for the best of reasons, or that politicians believe some of the promises they make, or that they actually come through on many. Perhaps some of us would like to believe in these ideals, as many people once did, but that is difficult when we are educated by the media to see the props behind the promise, the broad conceit of a media-driven political system—superimposed on a constitutional process—that masks modest but realistic possibilities for deliberation, incremental results, and in some instances good intentions.

The media are not likely to reveal this as a deceit because they take part in and benefit from the setup. Broadcast networks, cable operations, newspapers, magazines, and other media outlets are well served by the constant supply of sound bites, experts, and pictures that illustrate the dramatic and at times gripping stories of politics in the current age. Television in particular requires an unending supply of interesting visuals and conflictive story lines to ease the burden of needing the newest, most exciting, most graphic material. It appears, like the malevolent plant in *The Little Shop of Horrors,* to yell "Feed me!" to the handlers, book promoters—anyone whose self-interest can be packaged in colorful three-minute segments—all of whom happily comply as the medium grows ever larger and more destructive to the political process. Television, therefore, is a natural target for reformers seeking changes in the political process.

Yell it might and grow it will, but television is an unlikely vehicle for reform. It is an entertainment medium serving a political purpose. As such, it is somewhat miscast and will always do a better job at communicating the theatrical side of politics than the bland but essential give-and-take, interest-aggregation side that often gets displaced. Actually, as an entertainment medium, it does its job quite well. Politics is part performance; at its best, it can distract us while it teaches us something, much as a good play does. The problem lies not with the show but the role the show has come to play in the political system.

We are ill-served by television not because it does its job poorly but because it has assumed functions it is not designed to perform. Television is now the premiere vehicle for candidates to demonstrate their viability to potential contributors and stump for votes in primaries; political parties used to do that. It is the foremost method for presidents to amass public support for policy initiatives; grassroots campaigning once built those bonds. It is the mechanism of choice for members of Congress to decry the gridlock in their own institution, which was once more readily managed when party leaders held sway and members were far less visible.

At any rate, it's hard to imagine a medium seeking to change a situation from which it profits. Television may be miscast in the political system, and it may get bad reviews, but it also gets the viewers: a nine-figure audience for presidential debates; over 11 million for the Gore-Perot NAFTA face-off, the largest audience ever for "Larry King Live."[5] Coverage will continue to emphasize the controversial, negative, and unseemly side of politics and the mistakes and failures of politicians. It is, after all, entertaining. And people are watching. There is no incentive and, from an economic perspective, no need for change.

Neither are there strong incentives for journalists to change the system. In the television age, their celebrity status surpasses all previous professional expectations. Operating on the same stage as the politicians they make stars, the media's journalists, columnists, interviewers, and reporters indulge themselves in a sort of stardom unthinkable a generation ago. It's probably not hard to remember the last time you saw reporters playing themselves in a Hollywood movie, next to actors pretending to be politicians. Many reporters easily turn their newfound visibility into lucrative lecture fees, offering their punditry to trade associations that host celebrity speakers for a large cash return (Fallows, 1996). Hosts who interview celebrities become celebrities themselves. Larry King gets to interview Hillary Rodham Clinton, but then he gets to discuss the interview in *USA Today*, where he talks freely and in personal terms about his guest—and himself. "I saw a Hillary Clinton that I'd never seen before," says the interviewer turned chronicler. "She was funny, charming, sexy—yes, gang, sexy. We are both Scorpios, which tells you a lot" (October 4, 1993). What it tells you is that if the media counterrevolution comes, Larry King will not be leading the way.

To assert that television will not change is not to suggest that the medium or its role in politics is static. To the contrary, the very forces that worked to propel television into the political center ring are still in play. It is simply impossible to predict with great certainty what those changes will be or how they will affect the way politics is conducted.

Technological advances continue at staggering speeds. It is hard to say what 500-channel capability or interactive television will do to politics, although if the past decade is an accurate guide, it will likely intensify the present situation rather than alter it. If CNN offers the same perspective as its competitors, it is hard to imagine newer and perhaps narrower outlets (the Focus Group Channel?) doing otherwise. If politicians sell the appearance of interaction through town meetings, the ability to watch from a sofa may do more to advance the illusion than recreate the New England village green.

No matter how dramatic, these and other unanticipated developments probably will be evolutionary and reactive. Proactive change is more likely to come about from reformers tinkering with the rules of the game, a shift that could be more meaningful if it involves party rather than media reform. This may seem an odd claim, given the argument that party reform got us into the present situation. But if the media have become the default vehicle for performing functions that were better handled by parties, perhaps playing with the rules a bit more is not such a bad thing.

As constructed today, political parties are better suited to advocacy on behalf of individual candidates who can enlist a personal following than to public deliberation and compromise. This is in line with the one-way messages that are easily communicated on television and the interpersonal functions that are not. Political scientists Nelson Polsby and Aaron Wildavsky have assessed the consequences of this situation: "What is lost, in our view, is a capacity to deliberate, weigh competing demands, and compromise so that a variety of differing interests each gain a little" (Polsby and Wildavsky, 1980: p. 275).

Changing the criteria for selection and election could alter this situation. When candidacies were mediated by and funded through party organizations, candidates had to generate alliances with party leaders and interest groups that would carry into governance. Bargaining and compromise were essential. Although the decentralized nature of the system still frustrated initiative, victorious candidates came to office with alliances they could call upon to try to advance their agendas.

Unfortunately, the sort of reform necessary to reestablish parties as deliberative organizations will probably not occur, precisely because it looks bad on television. The original intent of the Democratic party reformers who gradually created the nomination-by-primary system was to open the process to rank-and-file partisans and to give minority voices in the party greater equality. By unintentionally making it harder for the party to negotiate among these voices, the reformers subjected the system to a generation of tinkering. If they never quite got it right, they certainly had the virtue of acting in the interests of openness and democracy.

Closing the system a bit is antidemocratic. It is hard to make the argument, especially in the age of the television town meeting, that a more centralized process could actually enhance the cause of democracy. After all, what could appear to be more egalitarian than a process that brings candidates into our homes via television, then lets us vote directly for them in primaries? It is easy to mistake talk shows for genuine deliberation, which makes it hard to argue that real deliberation is necessary.

People old enough to remember the political-machine era may envision the image of the closed smoke-filled rooms of pre-1968 politics, where a few over-weight middle-aged white men chomped on cigars and sweated profusely as they divided the spoils and determined among themselves who the party would nomi-nate. Aside from the nontrivial matter of the demographics, the process may not have been as closed as people think. Hal Bruno, now ABC News political director, was there and said, "The behind-the-scenes stuff is a bunch of mythology. Every-body knew what was happening behind the scenes, and reported it. The smoke-filled room had open windows, all over the place" (Kerbel, 1998: p. 212).

But it did not appear that way, and in a video era appearances are critical. Any effort to centralize and thereby strengthen political parties, should it come, would be hindered because it would not play well on television, which after all is about illusions. Watching the tube, we may be easily convinced that democracy is a sim-ple matter, just talking and voting. This makes television seem to be the most democratic instrument ever invented. Someone is always saying something, and remote control in hand, we can vote on whether we like it simply by pushing the channel-select button.

Of course, if it were this simple, we would expect people to feel efficacious, not discontented with the figures on the screen. Nonetheless, it is difficult to ask peo-ple to consider the peculiar logic that any system lacking the openness of Oprah could possibly be good for democracy. Pictures are convincing. But in the end, knowledge may be our best source of positive change. If altering the structure of television will not address what's wrong with the system, and if reverse party re-form is an academic's dream, our best hope, ultimately, is to educate ourselves to the meanings behind political messages.

## Conclusion

There is hope for this type of self-education, but it will take awareness and some work. People have been known to catch on to what the media feed them and, in some instances, to act up. Prior to the 1992 New York primary, Phil Donahue was bombarding his guest, the beleaguered governor of Arkansas, with pointed ques-tions about his personal life. Media scholar Kathleen Hall Jamieson recounts what happened next:

> Midway through Donahue's assault on Clinton, an exasperated candidate and an au-dience member both said, "Enough." "We're going to sit here a long time in silence, Phil. I'm not going to answer any more of these questions," said Clinton to rising au-dience applause. "I've answered 'em until I'm blue in the face. You are responsible for

the cynicism in this country. You don't want to talk about the real issues." As the crowd voiced its approval, an audience member agreed. "Given the pathetic state of most of the United States at this point . . . ," she said, "I can't believe you spent half an hour of air time attacking this man's character. I'm not even a Bill Clinton supporter, but I think this is ridiculous" (Jamieson, 1992: p. 265).

This audience member recognized the difference between attack journalism, which destroys, and aggressive journalism, which protects. With some consideration, we can too. Investigative reporting born of Watergate is a healthy thing for a nation; we are well served to know when our leaders are engaging in real crimes like obstruction of justice. But somewhere along the way the purpose got twisted. Today candidates are charged with the crime of seeking public office, of wishing to be at the same level as the journalists with whom they share the media stage.

In the children's tale, it took a child to tell the people what they inwardly knew: that their emperor wore no clothes. Good investigative reporting serves this purpose. Trivial reporting tells us about his underwear. Attack reporting tries to take it off.

We can tell the difference and thereby educate ourselves to the ways of politics and governance without falling prey to how the media frame events. But we have to remember that what we are looking at is only a picture in a frame: There are other angles, other dimensions, other shots. Even without seeing these other perspectives, we can find strength in knowing something else is there—that what we are being told about the political system is only one way of looking at it. Then we can make up our own minds about how to interpret what we learn in the media. We may find cause for cynicism nonetheless, but it will be an informed choice if we tread carefully and intelligently through the messages that surround the information we get. Politics, after all, is a buyer's market. Let the buyer beware.

# Discussion Questions

## Chapter 1
## Introduction: Under the President's Clothes

1. Consider some of your attitudes and feelings about politics and governance. How would you characterize the motivation and capability of candidates and elected officials? Upon what do you base your assessment?

2. In what ways and to what extent do the media influence our relationship to the political world? What factors might limit media influence?

3. How has the availability of political information changed over the past generation?

4. In recent years, people have come to rely on and trust television even as they express dissatisfaction with some aspects of coverage. How can you explain this apparent contradiction?

## Chapter 2
## Two Hundred Years of Politics and Reporting

1. Eisenhower and Nixon used what could be called deceptive practices to market their presidential candidacies. But their methods were used for different ends. Eisenhower hired advertising agents to enhance the image of a general with popular roots that was consistent with his history. Nixon used advertising to produce an image of an open, accessible candidate that was at odds with his persona. Is this difference significant? Is there an ethical difference between these objectives that makes the Nixon campaign more manipulative than the Eisenhower campaign, or does the inherently deceptive nature of advertising render the ends for which it is used irrelevant?

2. How have technological advances influenced the way candidates campaign for office and elected officials govern?

3. What lessons could be learned about the influence of television on governance from such episodes as the Kefauver organized crime hearings, the Murrow-McCarthy confrontation, and the Vietnam War?

4. Throughout American history, presidents and the press have needed and used each other. How did presidents like Thomas Jefferson, Theodore Roosevelt, Franklin D. Roosevelt, John F. Kennedy, and Ronald Reagan use the media to advance their agendas? How did reporters both benefit and suffer as a consequence of presidential efforts?

## Chapter 3
## A War of Words: Coverage of Politics and the Politics of Coverage

1. What do we mean when we say the media "frame" news of the election in a certain way? What are some predominant aspects of how the media frame stories about presidential candidates? What are the implications of media "frames" for the news/cynicism dilemma?

2. How did electoral and campaign finance reform combine to shift power from political party elites to the mass media in general and television in particular? In what respect has reform altered the characteristics of successful presidential candidates? On the basis of your analysis of the party elite–centered nomination system and the television-centered nomination system, which method of candidate selection would you say is more democratic, and why?

3. What does it mean when reporters engage in pack journalism and start a feeding frenzy? How might reporters frame a feeding frenzy in terms of the campaign horserace?

4. What messages are sent to the audience when campaign news emphasizes the words and actions of political advisers? The activities and experiences of political reporters?

5. The argument in Chapter 3 presupposes the public would be better served if political coverage deemphasized character allegations and personality issues. Do you agree with this assessment? Why or why not? What criteria should be used to determine whether a character allegation should be covered by reporters?

## Chapter 4
## Presidential Governance and Other Fantasies

1. How do constitutional expectations of governance differ from the version of governance portrayed in the media? How could this disparity affect the president? Congress? interest groups? the public?

2. How does coverage of policymaking parallel coverage of presidential campaigns? To what extent do you feel the parallels are appropriate? Why?

3. White House power struggles may be intensified under the glare of press scrutiny, a factor that arguably makes it more difficult for a president to govern. However, covering internal problems is consistent with a method of reporting that values openness; at one time, such conflicts were not widely covered, even though they were known to reporters. Which method do you believe better serves the public interest, and why?

4. How have congressional reform and the discovery of Congress by television changed the way Congress functions? Would the public be better served if media coverage emphasized lower congressional expectations? Different congressional expectations? Please explain your reasoning.

5. Why might media coverage of governance make it difficult for citizens to draw informed conclusions about what government does? To feel as if their opinions matter?

## Chapter 5
## What About Us?

1. The discussion in Chapter 5 suggests that the Internet and media outside the political mainstream do not offer suitable alternatives to the political frames offered by conventional journalists. What is the rationale for this argument? Do you agree or disagree, and why?

2. Televised "town meetings" are advertised as opportunities for people at home to interact with their national leaders. However, for most people, they are passive exercises in television watching. Are televised "town meetings" good or bad for democracy? Are they natural extensions of the participatory forums held in small communities or illusions that erroneously lead people to believe they are in touch with their government?

3. If the mainstream media send convergent messages about the motivation and behavior of politicians, and if serious news blends with popular culture, how can citizens acquire the information necessary to evaluate important political messages intelligently? Is journalistic reform a realistic solution to the dilemma? Political reform? Self-education? Why or why not?

4. How problematic is widespread cynicism about politics and politicians? One could argue that neither public opinion nor media coverage questions the basic legitimacy of government. However, one could counterargue that doubts raised about political actors and their motives are disincentives to important aspects of democracy, such as citizen participation. Which of these perspectives makes the most sense to you, and why?

# Glossary

**Agenda setting**   is one way the media influence the public by making people become aware of and think about issues and problems that are emphasized in the news.

**Apprenticeship**   was a norm of behavior in Congress for many years. Junior members were expected to work silently and eschew visibility. Congressional reforms instituted in the 1970s and the emergence of television undermined apprenticeship, giving junior members visibility and a greater voice in Congress.

**Campaign adviser,**   or handler, is an individual hired by a candidate to develop and coordinate an electoral strategy. Campaigns have employed advisers for many years; recently they have become the focus of media attention.

**Closed system**   describes the manner in which Congress conducted its business prior to the emergence of television and efforts to reform the institution in the 1970s. Under this system, power was centered around senior members in leadership positions, who functioned largely without public scrutiny.

**Delegates**   are individuals who attend national political party conventions in order to vote on the party's presidential and vice-presidential nominees and to draft the agenda, called a platform, that the nominees would pursue if elected. Most delegates are chosen in statewide primaries and arrive at the convention committed to a particular candidate.

**Demographic factors**   are group characteristics, such as race, gender, age, and education, that are descriptive of differences that influence why people select media and how they process political messages.

**Elites**   are small groups of individuals that wield power in organizations such as political parties. Until reform efforts undermined their control, political party elites could determine their party's presidential nominees.

**Federal Communications Commission (FCC)**   is a regulatory agency of the federal government with jurisdiction over broadcasting, including the power to grant or deny licenses to broadcast television and radio stations.

**Federal Election Campaign Act**   amendments of 1974 changed campaign financing by encouraging candidates to seek many small contributions. It also had the unintended effect of favoring presidential candidates who demonstrated their winning potential in early primaries.

**Federal matching funds**   are dollars provided to presidential candidates by the federal government equal in number to the value of private contributions of $250 or less. To be eligible for federal matching funds, candidates must agree to limit their overall spending. Candidates are not required to accept matching funds, although in practice only independently wealthy candidates like Ross Perot can afford to compete without federal money—thus avoiding the spending limits imposed when public money is accepted.

**Feeding frenzy**   describes how reporters will converge on a sensational story about a political figure and cover it relentlessly and to the exclusion of other news. Feeding frenzies are typically sparked by a public gaffe or rumor of an indiscretion by a candidate or official. The term conjures images of the press going after wounded politicians as a shark goes after injured prey.

**Frame**   refers to the perspective (or frame of reference) communicated by a news story that gives meaning to disparate facts and in turn influences how the reader or viewer understands the news. For instance, a story about the actions of a presidential candidate could be related in terms of his personal desire for power or his statesmanlike wish to promote the public good.

**Frontrunner**   is the perceived leader in an electoral contest such as a presidential primary. Reporters will determine who is leading the field by assessing which candidate has the most money, delegates, or support in opinion polls. Their evaluations constitute one element of horserace coverage.

**Going public**   is a term given to a presidential legislative strategy whereby presidents take their case for a policy initiative directly to the public via the media in an effort to pressure Congress with popular support.

**Governance**   is that portion of politics devoted to representing the public in which elected officials debate, develop, approve, and administer public policy.

**Horserace**   is the aspect of electoral politics that emphasizes competition. When reporters cover the horserace, they focus on measures of electability, such as which candidate has the most delegate votes, the most money, or the most support in public opinion polls.

**Infomercial**   is an advertisement in the form of a full-length, informative television program. In 1992, independent candidate Ross Perot built his presidential campaign around a series of infomercials, which he bankrolled with his personal fortune.

**Investigative reporting**   is when journalists aggressively seek to uncover scandalous events in prominent political and social institutions. The effectiveness of the *Washington Post* reporters Bob Woodward and Carl Bernstein in uncovering the Nixon administration Watergate scandal produced a generation of journalists committed to ferreting out and reporting wrongdoing.

**Lobbyists**   are agents of interest groups who represent their members by attempting to win favorable action on legislation. Although lobbyists may pressure members of Congress, their relationships with representatives are often cooperative.

The **McGovern-Fraser Commission**   was the first of several attempts by the Democratic party to make the presidential nomination process open and egalitarian, after the defeat of Hubert H. Humphrey in the 1968 election. The reforms had the intended effect of opening the process to rank-and-file voters but the unintended consequence of making television the predominant political link between candidates and voters.

**Mainstreaming** is the development of a common set of perceptions about the political and social world among heavy television viewers that are not held by light viewers with similar demographics. These mainstream perceptions reflect reality as it is portrayed on television.

**Media events** are staged activities performed for the purpose of attracting coverage in the press, particularly television. Once the domain of political campaigns, media events today are staged by elected officials as well.

**Medium** is a means of mass communication, such as television, newspapers, magazines, or radio. *Media* is the plural form.

The **New Hampshire primary** is traditionally the first primary held in a presidential election year.

**News management** is a deliberate effort by a candidate or official to get reporters to cover a particular matter in a favorable way.

The **North American Free Trade Agreement (NAFTA)** is a controversial pact providing for reduced exchange and investment barriers with Mexico and Canada. Negotiated by President Bush, it was ratified by Congress at the urging of President Clinton, despite sharp divisions in his Democratic party.

**Open system** describes the manner in which Congress conducted its business after the emergence of television and efforts to reform Congress in the 1970s. Under this system, the actions of Congress became visible to the public through media scrutiny.

**Pack journalism** is the tendency of reporters from different news organizations to follow each other's lead and approach the news from the same perspective. This is evident not only in the similar ways different media frame political news but also in the mob mentality exhibited by reporters when they engage in a "feeding frenzy" and saturate the media with details of a sensational story.

**Platforms** are statements drafted by political parties at their national conventions that detail the agenda their presidential nominee would pursue if elected.

**Political action committees (PACs)** are organizations established by interest groups for the purpose of raising and spending money on political candidates in the name of the establishing group.

**Political machines** were urban party organizations that dominated politics in many large American cities in the late nineteenth and early twentieth centuries. During this time, when the federal government did not provide welfare support, urban political leaders provided food, jobs, and services to people in exchange for their vote. Although people benefited in this manner, political machines were corrupt organizations that stifled political competition.

**Political party conventions** on the national level are gatherings held every four years for the purpose of nominating presidential and vice-presidential candidates and writing the platform that details the agenda they would pursue if elected.

**Political reporters** cover politics and elections. More than reporters who cover other subjects—such as foreign affairs, the economy, or the military—political reporters tend to be drawn to and report about the competition inherent in political events.

**Political socialization**  is the evolutionary process by which our attitudes toward and opinions of politics and government are shaped and developed. Although development may occur throughout one's lifetime, early childhood and adolescence are important stages in the political socialization of most people. Parents, siblings, peers, teachers, and the media all contribute to the process.

**Political spots**  are political advertisements, typically thirty- or sixty-second television ads.

**Politics**  describes the process by which political candidates and their assistants attempt to attain and hold public office. In the electoral setting, this includes engaging in a number of activities often commented upon by reporters, such as raising money, winning endorsements from public officials, running television advertisements, and pursuing a press strategy.

A **presidential primary**  is a statewide contest held for the purpose of selecting delegates to a political party convention. Not every state holds a primary, although in recent years the number of primaries has increased to the point that candidates can win enough delegates in primary contests to secure the nomination before the convention meets.

**Priming**  refers to a subtle effect of television on the viewing audience, noteworthy for its potential to influence the way viewers evaluate politicians on the basis of the context in which they are portrayed.

**Schema**  is a cognitive construct developed from direct or vicarious past experience that helps people organize information about the world.

**Self-referential coverage**  occurs when reporters mention themselves or their own concerns in the text of a news story. For political stories, this could include coverage of what it is like to cover a campaign, coverage of how reporters are treated by political officials, or coverage of how reporters battle politicians for control of the news agenda. Self-referential coverage often has a cynical cast.

**Seniority**  is the method used for many years to determine congressional leadership positions, whereby members with longer tenure would serve as committee chairs or ranking members of the minority party. Congressional reforms instituted in the 1970s modified the seniority system to give junior members a greater opportunity to wield power.

**Sound bite**  is a brief, continuous speech segment taken from an interview and broadcast in a television news report. During the 1988 presidential campaign, the average candidate sound bite was under ten seconds long.

**Spin**  refers to the emphasis political reporters place on the subjects they cover, which turns otherwise neutral information into a favorable or unfavorable story for a candidate or official. For instance, the neutral observation that a candidate finished second in a primary could be reported with a positive spin (by calling it "impressive") or a negative spin (by calling it "disappointing"). Political operatives are sometimes called "spin doctors" for their efforts to influence how the press will report a story.

**"Town meetings"**  are televised forums in which candidates or public officials such as the president answer questions from a studio audience of citizen participants and from callers watching at home. Modeled after community-based public meetings, they are a favorite venue of politicians seeking to avoid direct questioning by reporters while establishing the impression of access to a mass audience.

**Yellow journalism**   refers to a style of reporting popular in the late nineteenth and early twentieth centuries that featured lurid details of sensational stories complete with screaming headlines and eye-catching illustrations. The contemporary equivalent would be tabloid coverage of the sort found in newspapers like the *New York Post* and on television programs like "A Current Affair."

# Notes

## Chapter 1

1. On April 18, 1994.

2. See also Meyrowitz (1985), who argues that information is conveyed differently on television than in print because the medium is more expressive. He offers as an example that transcripts of the game show "Family Feud" would be boring to read, for they could not convey the reactions of the program's participants that give the show its vitality (p. 103).

3. Stanley and Niemi (1988). The figures are from this national survey question: "I'd like to ask you where you usually get most of your news about what's going on in the world today—from the newspapers or radio or television or magazines or talking to people or where?" Multiple responses were permitted.

4. Respondents were asked, "How would you rate the honesty and ethical standards of the people in these different fields—very high, high, average, low, or very low?" Television reporters were rated "average" by 50 percent; newspaper reporters, by 53 percent.

5. Respondents were asked, "In general, how would you rate the job the news media has done in covering the presidential campaign—excellent, good, only fair, or poor?" Fifty-five percent said "fair" or "poor."

6. Based on American National Election Study data and reported in Gallup (1993).

7. Information in this section comes from *Congressional Quarterly Weekly Report*, vol. 50, January 4 through February 15, 1992.

8. It should be noted that this discussion, like others in this book, addresses national politics. Whereas elements of running for national office, such as raising money and maintaining an effective organization, are important at all levels and to an extent will be the focus of coverage at all levels, some dynamics of state and local campaigns will differ from those described here.

9. "TV Coverage of Clinton Scandals" (Washington, DC: Center for Media and Public Affairs, 1998).

10. Some of the information in this section comes from a chronology of the Lewinsky scandal published on the CNN/Time AllPolitics Web site.

11. Information in this section comes from *Congressional Quarterly Weekly Report*, vol. 51, September 4 through November 20, 1993.

## Chapter 2

1. Diamond and Bates (1988), p. 53.

2. Halberstam (1993), p. 230.

3. Turner (1985) claims that Johnson specifically blamed television for undermining public support for the war.

4. Material in this section comes from the following sources: *Congress and the Nation,* vols. 5 and 7 (Washington, DC: Congressional Quarterly Press), 1981 and 1990; *Congressional Quarterly Weekly Report,* vol. 44, 1986.

5. The figure comes from the Annenberg Public Policy Center of the University of Pennsylvania. For a discussion of this and other points made in this section, see Kathleen Hall Jamieson, "Confused by Health-Care Ads? You Need a Field Guide," *Philadelphia Inquirer,* February 28, 1994.

## Chapter 3

1. Political scientist Theodore Lowi (1985) contends that parties were weakening prior to reform, which hastened but did not cause their decline. As evidence of party weakness, he argues that elites were unable to stave off the reformers.

2. The McGovern-Fraser Commission established the rules for 1972, the year George McGovern won the Democratic nomination. After McGovern's overwhelming defeat, reforms were attempted by the (Rep. Barbara) Mikulski Commission (for the 1976 election) and subsequently by the (Morley) Winograd Commission (1980), the (Gov. James) Hunt Commission (1984), and the Fairness Commission (1988).

3. Republicans also experienced changes in their nominating process during this time as more states held Republican primaries and conventions became ratifying mechanisms for primary choices. However, because Republicans constituted the incumbent party during most of the twenty-year period following 1968, the effects of reform were less contentious. See Peterson and Walker (1990).

4. Some observers (Wattenberg, 1982) believe the rise in the importance of television as a link between candidate and voter has hastened the decline of political parties.

5. National party chairs and senior party leaders do appear as sources and spokespersons in campaign coverage. But television emphasizes candidates far more than any other figures and largely disregards party leaders. Among institutions, the press, interest groups, and campaign organizations outnumbered parties among references made on select prime-time cable and network broadcasts during the 1992 campaign. See Kerbel (1998).

6. See, for instance, ABC's news coverage of Kerrey, Harkin, and Clinton advertising expenditures (February 14, 1992) and NBC's news coverage of Clinton's slide in the New Hampshire polls (February 15, 1992).

7. Center for Media and Public Affairs, Washington, DC.

8. For a discussion of why contemporary political coverage assumes a self-referential form, see Kerbel (1998), pp. 144–173.

9. Interestingly, some of the same technological advances that changed political reporting parallel those used by candidates to reach voters. See Smith (1986).

10. NBC's "Today" show hosted filmmakers D. A. Pennebaker and Chris Hegedus on October 28, 1993.

11. This, too, was reported in the press. See Newhouse News Service, October 6, 1992.

## Chapter 4

1. Political scientist Richard Neustadt (1990) analyzes the imprecise, variable quality of public prestige and its importance to presidential power.

2. Political scientist Theodore Lowi (1985) describes a "plebiscitary presidency," in which expectations of presidential performance are unrealistically inflated beyond the limits of institutional capability.

3. Paul Gigot of the *Wall Street Journal,* on CNN, "The McLaughlin Group," November 6, 1993.

4. Several prominent congressional scandals in recent years have received their share of media coverage. In 1994, House Ways and Means Committee chairman Dan Rostenkowski of Illinois was indicted for multiple alleged abuses of his power. During the same period, Senator Robert Packwood of Oregon was accused of sexual harassment by numerous women.

5. Quotations in this paragraph appeared on May 19, 1994.

## Chapter 5

1. Roderick Hart (1994) makes a similar argument, identifying "an inherent, technologically determined tension between television and politics since the former is meant to divert us and the latter to rivet us" (pp. 95–96).

2. For instance, Nina Totenberg asserted that controversy dogs Clinton because "the stories that he tells [about such things as his draft history] are ever so slightly different almost every time." Reported on National Public Radio, March 8, 1992.

3. A good example comes from a discussion with an NPR correspondent on CNN, who handicapped the NAFTA strategy this way: "The [administration's] idea was to beat one of their best friends [organized labor] to a pulp, and they found that they really couldn't do it." Mara Liasson on CNN, "Late Edition," November 7, 1993.

4. See, for instance, *Baltimore Sun,* February 11, 1992.

5. CNN release, November 10, 1993.

# References

Adatto, Kiku. 1990. "Sound Bite Democracy: Network Evening News Presidential Campaign Coverage, 1968 and 1988." Joan Shorenstein Barone Center on the Press, Politics, and Public Policy, Harvard University, Cambridge, MA. Research Paper R-2.

Alger, Dean E. 1989. *The Media and Politics.* Englewood Cliffs, NJ: Prentice-Hall.

Altheide, David L. 1976. *Creating Reality.* London: Sage Publications.

Asher, Herbert. 1980. *Presidential Elections and American Politics.* Homewood, IL: Dorsey Press.

Barilleaux, Ryan J. 1988. *The Post-Modern Presidency: The Office After Ronald Reagan.* New York: Praeger.

Berry, Jeffrey M. 1984. *The Interest Group Society.* Boston: Little, Brown.

Birnbaum, Jeffrey H. 1992. *The Lobbyists: How Influence Peddlers Get Their Way in Washington.* New York: Times Books.

Braestrup, Peter. 1983. *Big Story: How the American Press and Television Reported and Interpreted the Crisis of Tet 1968 in Vietnam and Washington.* New Haven: Yale University Press.

Burns, James MacGregor. 1956. *Roosevelt: The Lion and the Fox.* New York: Harcourt, Brace.

Carlson, James. 1985. *Prime Time Law Enforcement: Crime Show Viewing and Attitudes Toward the Criminal Justice System.* New York: Praeger.

Chester, Lewis, Godfrey Hodgson, and Bruce Page. 1969. *An American Melodrama: The Presidential Campaign of 1968.* New York: Viking Press.

Chester, Lewis, Cal McCrystal, Stephen Aris, and William Shawcross. 1973. *Watergate.* New York: Ballantine Books.

Cronin, Thomas E. 1980. *The State of the Presidency.* Boston: Little, Brown.

Danielian, Lucig H., and Benjamin I. Page. 1994. "The Heavenly Chorus: Interest Group Voices on TV News." *American Journal of Political Science* 38:1056–1078.

Diamond, Edwin, and Stephen Bates. 1988. *The Spot: The Rise of Political Advertising on Television.* Cambridge, MA: MIT Press.

Entman, Robert M. 1993. "Framing: Toward Clarification of a Fractured Paradigm." *Journal of Communication* 43:51–58.

Epstein, Edward J. 1973. *News from Nowhere: Television and the News.* New York: Vintage Books.

Exoo, Calvin F. 1994. *The Politics of the Mass Media.* Minneapolis: West Publishing.

Fallows, James. 1996. *Breaking the News: How the Media Undermine American Democracy.* New York: Pantheon Books.

Fishman, Mark. 1990. *Manufacturing the News.* Austin: University of Texas

Gallup, George, Jr. 1997. *The Gallup Poll 1996.* Wilmington, DE: Scholarly Resources, Inc.

_____. 1993. *The Gallup Poll 1992.* Wilmington, DE: Scholarly Resources, Inc.

Gans, Herbert. 1979. *Deciding What's News: A Study of CBS Evening News, NBC Nightly News, Newsweek, and Time.* New York: Random House.

Gerbner, George, Larry Gross, Michael Morgan, and Nancy Signorielli. 1984. "Political Correlates of Television Viewing." *Public Opinion Quarterly* 48:283–300.

_____. 1982. "Charting the Mainstream: Television's Contribution to Political Orientations." *Journal of Communication* 32:100–127.

_____. 1980a. "The 'Mainstreaming' of America: Violence Profile No. 11." *Journal of Communication* 30 (3):10–29.

_____. 1980b. "Aging with Television: Images on Television Drama and Conceptions of Social Reality." *Journal of Communication* 30 (1):37–47.

Gitlin, Todd. 1980. *The Whole World Is Watching: Mass Media in the Making and Unmaking of the New Left.* Berkeley: University of California Press.

Goffman, Erving. 1974. *Frame Analysis: An Essay on the Organization of Experience.* Cambridge, MA: Harvard University Press.

Graber, Doris A. 1993. *Mass Media and American Politics.* Washington, DC: Congressional Quarterly Press.

_____. 1988. *Processing the News: How People Tame the Information Tide.* New York: Longman.

Halberstam, David. 1993. *The Fifties.* New York: Villard Books.

Hallin, Daniel C. 1986. *The Uncensored War: The Media and Vietnam.* New York: Oxford University Press.

Hart, Roderick P. 1994. *Seducing America: How Television Charms the Modern Voter.* New York: Oxford University Press.

Hertsgaard, Mark. 1988. *On Bended Knee: The Press and the Reagan Presidency.* New York: Farrar, Straus & Giroux.

Iyengar, Shanto. 1996. "Framing Responsibility for Political Issues." *Annals of the AAPSS* 546:59–70.

_____. 1987. "Television News and Citizens' Explanations of National Affairs." *American Political Science Review* 81:815–831.

Iyengar, Shanto, and Donald R. Kinder. 1987. *News That Matters: Television and American Public Opinion.* Chicago: University of Chicago Press.

Jamieson, Kathleen Hall. 1992. *Dirty Politics: Deception, Distraction, and Democracy.* New York: Oxford University Press.

Joslyn, Richard. 1984. *Mass Media and Elections.* Reading, MA: Addison-Wesley.

Just, Marion, et al. 1996. *Crosstalk: Citizens, Candidates, and the Media in a Presidential Campaign.* Chicago: University of Chicago Press.

Just, Marion, Ann Crigler, and Lori Wallach. 1990. "Thirty Seconds or Thirty Minutes." *Journal of Communication* 40 (3):120–133.

Keeter, Scott, and Cliff Zukin. 1983. *Uninformed Choice: The Failure of the New Presidential Nominating System.* New York: Praeger.

Kellner, Douglas. 1990. *Television and the Crisis of Democracy.* Boulder, CO: Westview Press.

Kendrick, Alexander. 1969. *Prime Time: The Life of Edward R. Murrow.* Boston: Little Brown.

Kerbel, Matthew Robert. 1998. *Edited for Television: CNN, ABC, and American Presidential Elections.* Boulder, CO: Westview Press.

Kern, Montague, Patricia W. Levering, and Ralph B. Levering. 1983. *The Kennedy Crises: The Press, the Presidency, and Foreign Policy.* Chapel Hill: University of North Carolina Press.

Kernell, Samuel. 1986. *Going Public: New Strategies of Presidential Leadership.* Washington, DC: Congressional Quarterly Press.

Lowi, Theodore J. 1985. *The Personal President: Power Invested, Promise Unfulfilled.* Ithaca, NY: Cornell University Press.

———. 1969. *The End of Liberalism: Ideology, Policy, and the Crisis of Public Authority.* New York: W. W. Norton.

McCombs, Maxwell E., and Donald L. Shaw. 1972. "The Agenda-Setting Function of the Media." *Public Opinion Quarterly* 36:176–187.

McGinniss, Joe. 1969. *The Selling of the President 1968.* New York: Trident Press.

Maltese, John Anthony. 1992. *Spin Control: The White House Office of Communications and the Management of Presidential News.* Chapel Hill: University of North Carolina Press.

Mayhew, David R. 1975. *Congress: The Electoral Connection.* New Haven: Yale University Press.

Meyrowitz, Joshua. 1985. *No Sense of Place: The Impact of Electronic Media on Social Behavior.* New York: Oxford University Press.

Miller, Arthur H., Edie N. Goldenberg, and Lutz Erbring. 1979. "Type-Set Politics: Impact of Newspapers on Public Confidence." *American Political Science Review* 73:67–84.

Miller, Warren E., Donald R. Kinder, and Steven J. Rosenstone. 1996. *American National Election Study, 1996.* Ann Arbor, MI: Inter-University Consortium for Political and Social Research.

———. 1993. *American National Election Study, 1992.* Ann Arbor, MI: Inter-University Consortium for Political and Social Research.

Morgan, Michael. 1989. "Television and Democracy." In Ian Angus and Sut Jhally, eds., *Cultural Politics in Contemporary America.* New York: Routledge.

———. 1982. "Television and Adolescents' Sex Role Stereotypes: A Longitudinal Study." *Journal of Personality and Social Psychology* 43:947–955.

Neuman, W. Russell, Marion R. Just, and Ann N. Crigler. 1992. *Common Knowledge: News and the Construction of Political Meaning.* Chicago: University of Chicago Press.

Neustadt, Richard. 1990. *Presidential Power and the Modern Presidents.* New York: Free Press.

Ornstein, Norman J. 1983. "The Open Congress Meets the President." In Anthony King, ed., *Both Ends of the Avenue: The Presidency, the Executive Branch, and Congress in the 1980s.* Washington, DC: American Enterprise Institute.

Owen, Diana. 1993. "Politics and 'The Last Frontier': The Talk Radio Audience and the 1992 Presidential Election." Paper presented at the annual meeting of the Midwest Political Science Association, Chicago.

Page, Benjamin I., Robert Y. Shapiro, and Glenn R. Dempsey. 1987. "What Moves Public Opinion?" *American Political Science Review* 81:23–43.

Parenti, Michael. 1993. *Inventing Reality: The Politics of the News Media.* New York: St. Martin's Press.

Patterson, Thomas E. 1993. *Out of Order.* New York: Alfred A. Knopf.

———. 1980. *The Mass Media Election: How Americans Choose Their President.* New York: Praeger.

Patterson, Thomas E., and Robert D. McClure. 1976. *The Unseeing Eye: The Myth of Television Power in National Politics.* New York: Putnam.

Peterson, Mark A., and Jack L. Walker. 1990. "The Presidency and the Nominating System." In Michael Nelson, ed., *The Presidency and the Political System.* 3d ed. Washington, DC: Congressional Quarterly Press.

Polsby, Nelson W. 1983. "Some Landmarks in Modern Presidential-Congressional Relations." In Anthony King, ed., *Both Ends of the Avenue: The Presidency, the Executive Branch, and Congress in the 1980s.* Washington, DC: American Enterprise Institute.

Polsby, Nelson W., and Aaron Wildavsky. 1980. *Presidential Elections: Strategies of American Electoral Politics.* New York: Charles Scribner's, Inc.

Pomper, Gerald M. 1973. *Elections in America: Control and Influence in Democratic Politics.* New York: Dodd, Mead.

Popkin, Samuel L. 1991. *The Reasoning Voter: Communication and Persuasion in Presidential Campaigns.* Chicago: University of Chicago Press.

Ranney, Austin. 1983. *Channels of Power: The Impact of Television on American Politics.* New York: Basic Books.

Reedy, George E. 1987. *The Twilight of the Presidency.* New York: Mentor Books.

Ripley, Randall B. 1983. *Congress: Process and Policy.* 3d ed. New York: W. W. Norton.

Robinson, Michael J., and Margaret A. Sheehan. 1983. *Over the Wire and on TV: CB and UPI in Campaign '80.* New York: Russell Sage Foundation.

Rubin, Richard L. 1981. *Press, Party, and Presidency.* New York: W. W. Norton.

Sabato, Larry J. 1991. *Feeding Frenzy: How Attack Journalism Has Transformed American Politics.* New York: Free Press.

Sanders, Elizabeth. 1990. "The Presidency and the Bureaucratic State." In Michael Nelson, ed., *The Presidency and the Political System.* 3d ed. Washington, DC: Congressional Quarterly Press.

Schlesinger, Arthur M., Jr. 1965. *A Thousand Days: John F. Kennedy in the White House.* Boston: Houghton Mifflin.

Schoenbrun, David. 1989. *On and Off the Air: An Informal History of CBS News.* New York: E. P. Dutton.

Schram, Martin. 1987. *The Great American Video Game: Presidential Politics in the Television Age.* New York: William Morrow.

_____. 1977. *Running for President 1976: The Carter Campaign.* New York: Stein and Day.

Seib, Philip M. 1987. *Who's in Charge? How the Media Shape News and Politicians Win Votes.* Dallas: Taylor Publishing.

Smith, Robert. 1986. "New Technologies in Campaigns." In L. Patrick Devlin, ed., *Political Persuasion in Presidential Campaigns.* New Brunswick, NJ: Transaction Books.

Smoller, Fred. 1986. "The Six O'Clock Presidency: Patterns of Network News Coverage of the President." *Presidential Studies Quarterly* 16:31–49.

Stanley, Harold, and Richard Niemi. 1994. *Vital Statistics on American Politics.* Washington, DC: Congressional Quarterly Press.

_____. 1988. *Vital Statistics on American Politics.* Washington, DC: Congressional Quarterly Press.

Stroud, Kandy. 1977. *How Jimmy Won: The Victory Campaign from Plains to the White House.* New York: William Morrow.

Stuckey, Mary E. 1991. *The President as Interpreter-in-Chief.* Chatham, NJ: Chatham House.

Truman, David B. 1955. *The Governmental Process.* New York: Knopf.

Tuchman, Gaye. 1978. *Making News: A Study in the Construction of Reality.* New York: Free Press.

Tulis, Jeffrey K. 1987. *The Rhetorical Presidency.* Princeton, NJ: Princeton University Press.

Turner, Kathleen J. 1985. *Lyndon Johnson's Dual War: Vietnam and the Press.* Chicago: University of Chicago Press.

Volgy, Thomas J., and John E. Schwarz. 1980. "TV Entertainment Programming and Sociopolitical Attitudes." *Journalism Quarterly* 57:150–155.

Walker, Jack L., Jr. 1991. *Mobilizing Interest Groups in America.* Ann Arbor: University of Michigan Press.

Watson, Mary Ann. 1990. *The Expanding Vista: American Television in the Kennedy Years.* New York: Oxford University Press.

Wattenberg, Martin P. 1982. "From Parties to Candidates: Examining the Role of the Media." *Public Opinion Quarterly* 46:216–227.

West, Darrell M. 1993. *Air Wars: Television Advertising in Election Campaigns, 1952–1992.* Washington, DC: Congressional Quarterly Press.

White, Graham J. 1979. *FDR and the Press.* Chicago: University of Chicago Press.

Winfield, Betty Houchin. 1990. *FDR and the News Media.* Urbana: University of Illinois Press.

Woodward, Bob. 1994. *The Agenda: Inside the Clinton White House.* New York: Simon and Schuster.

Wyatt, Clarence R. 1993. *Paper Soldiers: The American Press and the Vietnam War.* New York: W. W. Norton.

# Index